Guided Math Lessons in Fourth Grade

Guided Math Lessons in Fourth Grade provides detailed lessons to help you bring guided math groups to life. Based on the bestselling *Guided Math in Action*, this practical book offers 16 lessons, taught in a round of three—concrete, pictorial and abstract. The lessons are based on the priority standards and cover fluency, word problems, fractions and place value. Author Dr. Nicki Newton shows you the content as well as the practices and processes that should be worked on in the lessons, so that students not only learn the content but also how to solve problems, reason, communicate their thinking, model, use tools, use precise language, and see structure and patterns.

Throughout the book, you'll find tools, templates and blackline masters so that you can instantly adapt the lesson to your specific needs and use it right away. With the easy-to-follow plans in this book, students can work more effectively in small guided math groups—and have loads of fun along the way! Remember that guided math groups are about doing the math. So throughout these lessons you will see students working with manipulatives to make meaning, doing mathematical sketches to show what they understand and can make sense of the abstract numbers. When students are given the opportunities to make sense of the math in hands-on and visual ways, then the math begins to make sense to them!

Dr. Nicki Newton has been an educator for 30 years, working both nationally and internationally with students of all ages. She has worked on developing Math Workshop and Guided Math Institutes around the country; visit her website at www.drnickinewton.com. She is also an avid blogger (www.guidedmath.wordpress.com), tweeter (@drnickimath) and Pinterest pinner (www.pinterest.com/drnicki7).

Guided Math Lessons in Fourth Grade

Getting Started

Dr. Nicki Newton

Routledge
Taylor & Francis Group

NEW YORK AND LONDON

First published 2022
by Routledge
605 Third Avenue, New York, NY 10158

and by Routledge
2 Park Square, Milton Park, Abingdon, Oxon, OX14 4RN

Routledge is an imprint of the Taylor & Francis Group, an informa business

Library of Congress Cataloging-in-Publication Data
A catalog record for this book has been requested

ISBN: 978-0-367-77057-0 (hbk)
ISBN: 978-0-367-76002-1 (pbk)
ISBN: 978-1-003-16958-1 (ebk)

DOI: 10.4324/9781003169581

Typeset in Palatino
by Apex CoVantage, LLC

Contents

Acknowledgments

I thank God for life and happiness. I thank my family and friends for all their support. I thank my editor Lauren who is the best in the world! I thank all the reviewers who gave feedback that helped make the series what it is! I thank the copyediting and production team for all their hard work.

I would also like to thank Math Learning Center (www.mathlearningcenter.org/apps), Braining Camp (www.brainingcamp.com/) and Didax (www.didax.com/math/virtual-manipulatives.html) for the use of screenshots of their fabulous virtual manipulatives.

www.brainingcamp.com/
www.mathlearningcenter.org/apps

Meet the Author

Dr. Nicki Newton has been an educator for over 30 years, working both nationally and internationally, with students of all ages. Having spent the first part of her career as a literacy and social studies specialist, she built on those frameworks to inform her math work. She believes that math is intricately intertwined with reading, writing, listening and speaking. She has worked on developing Math Workshop and Guided Math Institutes around the country. Most recently, she has been helping districts and schools nationwide to integrate their State Standards for Mathematics and think deeply about how to teach these within a math workshop model. Dr. Nicki works with teachers, coaches and administrators to make math come alive by considering the powerful impact of building a community of mathematicians who make meaning of real math together. When students do real math, they learn it. They own it, they understand it, and they can do it. Every one of them. Dr. Nicki is also an avid blogger (www. guidedmath.wordpress. com), tweeter (@drnickimath) and Pinterest pinner (www.pinterest. com/drnicki7/). She speaks around the country and will virtually pop into any bookstudy if requested!

Contact her at:
Dr. Nicki Newton, Educational Consultant
Phone: 347–688–4927
Email: drnicki7@gmail.com

Find More Online!

Resources, videos and conversations with Dr. Nicki can be found in the Guided Math Dropbox Resources: https://bit.ly/2Ja4sMY

1

Introduction

Figure 1.1 Guided Math Example 1

I pull a group of 4th graders who are working on dividing a two-digit number by a one-digit number. We are working on building conceptual understanding. We are using place value blocks to explore the concept.

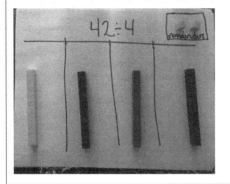

Figure 1.2 Guided Math Example 2

I pull a different group who is working on the same concept. We are working on modeling with open arrays. Students are each picking a problem and modeling it out and sharing their thinking with the group.

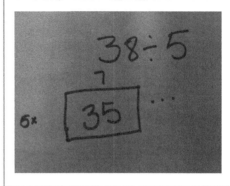

Guided math is a small group instructional strategy that teaches students in their zone of proximal development around the priority standards (see Figures 1.1 and 1.2). There are so many standards, but every state has priority focus standards. Those are the standards that you teach in a small guided math group. It is a time for hands-on, minds-on learning based on the standards. It is a time for discussing ideas, listening to the thinking of others, reasoning out loud and becoming a confident, competent mathematician.

Guided math groups are for everyone! Too often, students are rushed through big ideas, understandings and skills. They are left with ever widening gaps. Guided math groups give teachers the time needed to work with students in a way that they can all learn. Guided math groups can be used to remediate, to teach on grade level concepts and to address the needs of students who are working beyond grade level.

There are different ways that students can be grouped. Sometimes students are grouped by readiness. Other times students are grouped by interest or choice. So, for example, say you are working on rounding and half the class gets it and the other half is still struggling. You might pull some temporary small groups and practice some hands-on lessons with the beaded number line for the students who are struggling, but that doesn't mean you will forget about the other kids. You could also pull another group of kids and play a rounding card game (they are past needing the concrete scaffolds). You could have days where you pull a heterogeneous group and allow the kids who need the scaffolds to use them during the game (see Figures 1.3 and 1.4).

DOI: 10.4324/9781003169581-1

Figure 1.3 Visually Leveled Flashcards   **Figure 1.4** Number Line

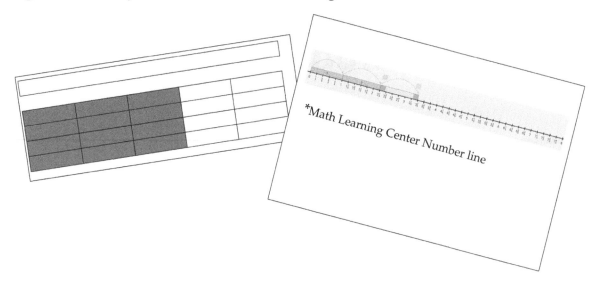

*Math Learning Center Number line

You could also ask students what they are interested in working on in small groups. You all would have a whole class discussion and generate a list of topics and then students would sign up for groups sessions that they are interested in attending. The focus here is that the students generate the topics and then sign up for them. Another way to do this is to have the teacher think about different topics that the students need to work on, based on the data and then offer those topics to the students, and they can sign up for which sessions that they want to attend.

Guided math groups can be heterogeneous or homogeneous. It depends on what you are trying to do. If you are teaching a specific skill, such as multiplying by 4's, one group could be working with visually leveled flashcards and another group could be working with more abstract number flashcards. You could also pull a group that is still exploring it just concretely on the beaded number line for another session. The groups are flexible and students work in different groups at different times, never attached to any one group for the entire year. Students meet in a particular guided math group for three or four times based on their specific instructional needs and then they move on.

Guided math groups can occur in all types of classrooms. Typically, they are part of a math workshop. In a math workshop (see Figure 1.5) there are three parts.

Opening	Student Activity	Debrief
♦ Energizers and routines	♦ Math workstations	♦ Discussion
♦ Problem solving	♦ Guided math groups	♦ Exit Slip
♦ Mini-lesson		♦ Mathematician's chair share

What Are the Other Kids Doing?

The other students should be engaged in some type of independent practice. They can be working alone, with partners or in small groups. They could be rotating through stations based on a designated schedule or they could be working from a menu of Must Do's and Can Do's. The point is that students should be practicing fluency, word problems, place value and working on items in the current unit of study. This work should be organized in a way that students are working in their zone of proximal development (Vygotsky, 1978).

Figure 1.5 Math Workshop

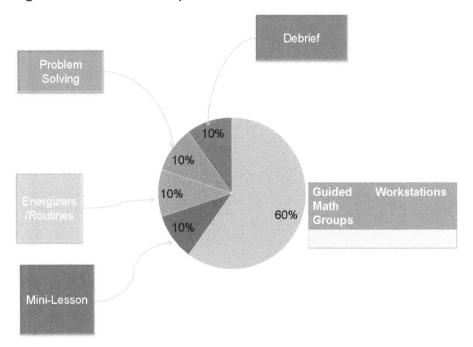

Differentiating workstations helps to purposefully plan for the learning of all students (see Figures 1.6 and 1.7). For example, the fluency workstation games should be divided by strategy; for examples students can be working on different strategies, some working on addition doubles plus 1, others on doubling with multiplication tables (Baroody, 2006; Van de Walle & Lovin, 2006; Henry & Brown, 2008). Another example is word problems. There are 9 different types of multiplication and division problems. Different students might be working on different structures. For example, some students might be working on equal group problems, while others are working on multiplicative comparison problems. The goal is that by the end of the year they all know all the types. Knowing the learning trajectory and understanding the structures that go from simple to complex can help organize the teaching and learning of word problems (Carpenter, Fennema, Franke, Levi, & Empson, 1999/2015; Fuchs et al., 2010); Jitendra, Hoff, & Beck (1999) (see Figure 1.8).

Figures 1.6 & **1.7** Workstation Games

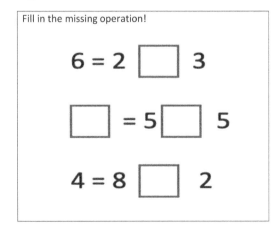

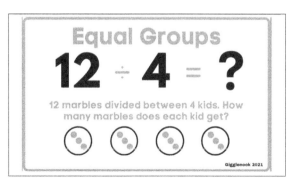

Figure 1.8 Workstation Contract

Workstation Contract

I have the privilege of learning with the Math Workstations.

I will play fair.

I will be a good sport. If I win, I will celebrate appropriately. If I lose, I'll be a good sport.

I will use the math manipulatives the way they are supposed to be used.

I will use the digital resources the way they are supposed to be used.

I will put everything back neatly.

I will work hard every day.

I will keep trying when the going gets tough!

My Signature:_____

Date: _____

Benefits of Guided Math Groups

♦ See student knowledge in action
♦ Monitor the concepts and skills that are understood
♦ Catch and address the misunderstandings
♦ Ask questions that highlight thinking
♦ Analyze thinking
♦ Listen to conversations
♦ Assess in the moment
♦ Redirect in the moment
♦ Differentiate as needed

Key Points

♦ Different reasons: remediate, focus on grade level topics or working beyond grade level
♦ Cycle of engagement: concrete, pictorial, abstract
♦ Heterogeneous and homogeneous grouping
♦ Math workshop
♦ Math workstations
♦ Benefits of guided math

Chapter Summary

Guided math is a great way to differentiate learning for all your students. Focus on the priority standards. Students approach these standards through a concrete, pictorial and abstract cycle of engagement. Sometimes, the groups are homogeneous groups, and other times the groups are heterogeneous. Guided math groups can be done in a variety of ways, either traditional set-ups or a math workshop model. The other students should always be doing work that they are familiar with and are practicing in the math workstation. Many times, the work that students are working on in the guided math group is carried over into the math workstation. When the students are in guided math groups, the other students should be meaningfully engaged in math workstations. All of this works together to give all students a chance to learn.

Reflection Questions

1. How are you differentiating instruction around the priority standards right now?
2. Currently, how do you group students? What informs your grouping?
3. Do you have a plan to make sure that everybody fully understands the priority standards?

References

Baroody, A. J. (2006). Why children have difficulties mastering the basic number combinations and how to help them. *Teaching Children Mathematics, 13*, 22–32.

Carpenter, T. P., Fennema, E., Franke, M. L., Levi, L., & Empson, S. B. (2015). *Children's mathematics: Cognitively guided instruction*. NH: Heinemann.

Fuchs, L., Zumeta, R., Schumacher, R., Powell, S., Seethaler, P., Hamlett, C., & Fuchs, D. (2010). The effects of schema-broadening instruction on second graders' word-problem performance and their ability to represent word problems with algebraic equations: A randomized control study. *Elementary School Journal, 110*(4), 446–463. Retrieved January 4, 2020 from https://www.ncbi.nlm.nih.gov/pubmed/20539822

Henry, V., & Brown, R. (2008, March). First-grade basics: An investigation into teaching and learning of an accelerated, high-demand memorization standard. *Journal for Research in Mathematics Education, 39*(2), 153–183.

Jitendra, A. K., Hoff, K., & Beck, M. M. (1999). Teaching middle school students with learning disabilities to solve word problems using a schema-based approach. *Remedial and Special Education, 20*(1), 50–64. https://doi.org/10.1177/074193259902000108

Van de Walle, J. A., & Lovin, L. A. H. (2006). *Teaching student-centered mathematics: Grades 3–5.* Boston: Pearson.

Vygotsky, L. S. (1978). *Mind in society: The development of higher psychological processes.* Cambridge, MA: Harvard University Press.

2
Behind the Scenes

Assessment

Assessment is a crucial element in designing a guided math lesson. Teachers have to know where their students are along the trajectory of learning so that they can plan to teach them purposefully. Teachers need actionable data. Actionable data is data that can be used immediately to develop meaningful lessons. At the beginning of the year, teachers need to get data about the priority standards/major cluster standards from the year before so they can figure out if there are any gaps and make a plan to close them. Richardson notes, "The information gathered from the assessments helps teachers pinpoint what each child knows and still needs to learn. They are not about 'helping children be right,' but about uncovering their instructional needs (n.d.)."

Math Running Records is a great way to check fluency! It's the GPS of fact fluency (see Figure 2.1). Remember every summer, students lose 2.6 months of math at least (Shafer, 2016). Teachers should assess fluency, word problems, operations and algebraic thinking and place value in the beginning of the year. At the middle of the year, teachers should assess all the grade level work done in these areas during the first part of the year. At the end of the year, teachers should assess all the priority standards for the grade. Throughout the year, teachers should rely on entrance and exit slips (Figure 2.2), quizzes, anecdotes, unit assessments and conferring to get information about students.

Grouping

Guided math groups should have three to five students. Sometimes they are heterogeneous groups, and sometimes they are homogeneous groups. It depends on what you are trying to do. If you are working on big ideas and understanding, you might pull a small group of students and have them work on modeling with different tools. You might pull students together and work on some word problems. However, if you are working on multiplication basic facts and you are working on a specific strategy, you might pull a group that is working on relating the 2's, 4's and 8's. You might pull another group that you are working on square numbers with. Groups should last between 10 and 15 minutes. Remember the attention span rule: age plus a few minutes.

Differentiation

After teachers get the data, they need to use it to differentiate (see Figure 2.1). Some of the work is to close the gaps. Some of the work is to accelerate the learning of the advanced students. Some of the work is to teach in the grade level zone. A big part of the differentiation aspect of guided math lessons is the concrete, pictorial and abstract cycle. Sometimes, students know the answer but do not necessarily understand the math. It is crucial to do quick assessments with students to make sure that they understand the math. For example, students might know the 8 multiplication facts

DOI: 10.4324/9781003169581-2

Figure 2.1 Math Running Records Example

Addition Running Record Recording Sheet

Student: _____ Teacher:_____ Date: _____

Part 1: Initial Observations
Teacher: We are now going to administer Part 1 of the Running Record. I am going to give you a sheet of paper with some problems. I want you to go from the top to the bottom and tell me just the answer. If you get stuck, you can stop and ask for what you need to help you. If you want to pass, you can. We might not do all of the problems. I am going to take notes so I remember what happened. Let's start.

Part 1	Codes: What do you notice?	Initial Observations of Strategies	Data Code Names
0 + 1 a 5s pth	ca fco cah coh wo sc asc dk	0 1 2 3 4M 4	A0----- add 0
2 + 1 a 5s pth	ca fco cah coh wo sc asc dk	0 1 2 3 4M 4	A1----- add 1
3 + 2 a 5s pth	ca fco cah coh wo sc asc dk	0 1 2 3 4M 4	Aw5--- add w/in 5
2 + 6 a 5s pth	ca fco cah coh wo sc asc dk	0 1 2 3 4M 4	Aw10 add w/in 10
4 + 6 a 5s pth	ca fco cah coh wo sc asc dk	0 1 2 3 4M 4	AM10---add making 10
10 + 4 a 5s pth	ca fco cah coh wo sc asc dk	0 1 2 3 4M 4	A10-----add 10 to a #
7 + 7 a 5s pth	ca fco cah coh wo sc asc dk	0 1 2 3 4M 4	AD------add doubles
5 + 6 a 5s pth	ca fco cah coh wo sc asc dk	0 1 2 3 4M 4	AD1-----add dbls +/-1
7 + 5 a 5s pth	ca fco cah coh wo sc asc dk	0 1 2 3 4M 4	AD2----add dbls +/-2
9 + 6 a 5s pth	ca fco cah coh wo sc asc dk	0 1 2 3 4M 4	AHF/C9-add higher facts use compensation w/9
8 + 4 a 5s pth	ca fco cah coh wo sc asc dk	0 1 2 3 4M 4	AHF/C7/8 add higher facts/use compensation with 7/8
7 + 8 a 5s pth	ca fco cah coh wo sc asc dk	0 1 2 3 4M 4	AHF/C7/8 add higher facts/use compensation with 7/8
Codes a - automatic 5s - 5 seconds pth - prolonged thinking time	**Types of Strategies** ca – counted all fco – finger counted on cah counted all in head coh counted on in head wo - wrong operation sc – self corrected asc – attempted to self-correct dk – didn't know	**Strategy Levels** 0 – doesn't know 1 – counting strategies by ones or skip counting using fingers, drawings or manipulatives 2 - mental math/solving in head 3 - using known facts and strategies 4M - automatic recall from memory 4 – automatic recall and students have number sense	

Figure 2.1 (Continued)

Part 2: Flexibility/Efficiency

Teacher: We are now going to administer Part 2 of the Running Record. In this part of the Running Record we are going to talk about what strategies you use when you are solving basic addition facts. I am going to tell you a problem and then ask you to tell me how you think about it. I am also going to ask you about some different types of facts. Take your time as you answer and tell me what you are thinking as you see and do the math. I am going to take notes so I can remember everything that happened during this Running Record.

Add 0 0 + 1	Add 1 2 + 1	Add w/in 5 or 10 3 + 2 2 + 6	Add to Make 10 4 + 6
What happens when you add zero to a number? ___ same # __ other ___ can't articulate	What strategy do you use when you add 1 to a number? ___ next counting # __ other ___ can't articulate	How do you solve 4 + 0? And 6 + 3? ___ count on from big # __ other ___ can't articulate	How do you solve 5 + 5? ___ count on from big # __ other ___ can't articulate
What would be the answer to.. 3 + 0 0 + 5 8 + 0	What would be the answer to ... 4 + 1 1 + 7 10 + 1	w/in 5 w/in 10 1 + 3 5 + 4 2 + 2 2 + 7	i'm going give you a number and I want you to give me the number that makes 10 with it. If I give you 7, how many more to make 10? If I give you __ how many more to 10? 9? 2? 6? 3?
Do they know this strategy? No/Emerging/Yes A0 Level 0 1 2 3 4M 4	Do they know this strategy? No/Emerging/Yes A1 Level 0 1 2 3 4M 4	Do they know this strategy? No/Emerging/Yes A10 Level 0 1 2 3 4M 4	Do they know this strategy? No/Emerging/Yes AM10 Level 0 1 2 3 4M 4
Add 10 10 + 4	**Doubles 7 + 7**	**Doubles +/- 1 5 + 6**	**Doubles +/- 2 7 + 5**
What strategy do you use when you add 10 to a number? ___ teen #s decompose to 10 and 1's __other __ can't articulate	How would you solve 6 + 6? ___ doubles ___ other __ can't articulate	How would you solve 6 + 7? ___ doubles +/-1 ___ other __ can't articulate	If a friend did not know how to solve 7 + 9, what would you tell her to do? ___ doubles +/-2 __other __ can't articulate
How would you solve? 10 + 2 10 + 6 10 + 8	How would you solve? 4 + 4 8 + 8 9 + 9 What kind of facts are these?	How would you solve? 2 + 3 3 + 4 8 + 9	How would you solve? 2 + 4 8 + 6 9 + 11
Do they know this strategy?	_____ Do they know this strategy?	Do they know this strategy?	Do they know this strategy?
No/Emerging/Yes A10 Level 0 1 2 3 4M 4	No/Emerging/Yes AD Level 0 1 2 3 4M 4	No/Emerging/Yes AD1 Level 0 1 2 3 4M 4	No/Emerging/Yes AD2 Level 0 1 2 3 4M 4

(*Continued*)

Figure 2.1 (Continued)

Bridge through 10 (9) 9 + 6	Bridge through 10 (7/8) 8 + 4	Part 3: Mathematical Disposition
If your friend was stuck solving 9 + 5, what would you tell him to do? ___ bridge 10 ___other ___ can't articulate How do you solve_____? 9 + 3 9 + 6 Do they know this strategy? No/Emerging/Yes AHF/C9 Level 0 1 2 3 4M 4	What strategy would you use to solve 8 + 3? ___ bridge 10 ___other ___ can't articulate How would you solve__? 4 + 7? 8 + 5? Do they know this strategy? No/Emerging/Yes AHF/C 7/8 Level 0 1 2 3 4M 4	Do you like math? What do you find easy? What do you find tricky? What do you do when you get stuck?

Part 3 continued
Question Prompts:
That's interesting/fascinating: tell me what you did.
That's interesting/fascinating: tell me how you solved it.
That's interesting/fascinating: tell me what you were thinking.
How did you solve this problem?
Can you tell me more about how you solve these types of problems?
What do you mean when you say__? (i.e. ten friends/neighbor numbers etc.)

General Observations (to be filled out after the interview)

Instructional Response:
Fluency Focus areas (circle all that apply): flexibility   efficiency   accuracy   automaticity

What addition strategy should the instruction focus on?

A0 A1 Aw5 Aw10 AM10 A10 AD AD1 AD2 AHF/C9 AHF/C 7/8

For his/her current instructional level, what is the predominant way in which the student is arriving at the answers? 0 1 2 3 4M 4 _____

Overall, what is the way in which the students calculated the answers?: 0 1 2 3 4M 4

Comments/Notes about gestures, behaviors, remarks:

*In most states k fluency is within 5 and 1st grade fluency is within 10 and 2nd grade within 20. However, some states k is within 10 and 1st and 2nd is within 20.

Figure 2.2 Exit Slip Example

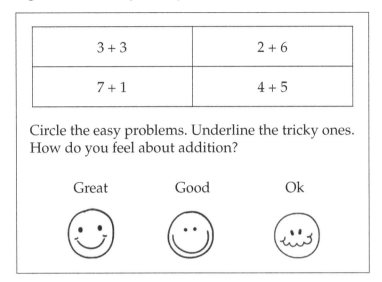

3 + 3	2 + 6
7 + 1	4 + 5

Circle the easy problems. Underline the tricky ones.
How do you feel about addition?

Great   Good   Ok

by skip counting by 8's. So, they can get an answer but they don't have strategic competence. We want them to have flexibility and efficiency with numbers, for example in this case thinking I can double my 4's or another efficient strategy. We would practice it in a variety of ways with manipulatives, with sketches and with the numbers. We would also have the students verbalize what they are doing and contextualize it by telling stories (NCTM, 2014) (see Figure 2.3).

Figure 2.3 Differentiated Workstations

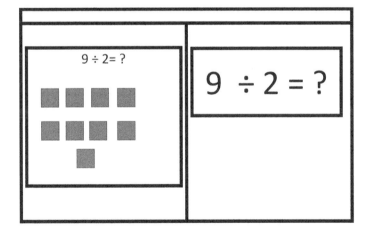

$9 \div 2 = ?$

$$9 \div 2 = ?$$

Types of Groups

When we are thinking about grouping, it is about meeting the needs of the students where they are and taking them to what they need to learn at that grade level, so students are emerging in their learning along the continuum. It is about creating flexible groups that students can move through as they work on different concepts. These groups should never be "fixed" and track students throughout the year. They are temporary, flexible and focused groups that teach students what they need, when they need it and then students move on to different work (see Figure 2.4).

Figure 2.4 Types of Groups

Group 1: Emergent	Group 2: Early Fluent	Group 3: Fluent	Group 4: Advanced Fluent
These are the students who are working below grade level in some areas. They have many strengths but also they often have many gaps and misunderstandings. It is important to work on closing gaps as well as highly scaffolding (but not overscaffolding) current grade level material.	These students are approaching grade level. They know some stuff and they are shaky on other things. They have some gaps and need some remediation.	These students are right at grade level. Sometimes, these students have a limited understanding of the math. Oftentimes, they can get the answer but they have trouble explaining what they did and why they did it.	These students are working above grade level. This doesn't mean that the work should be done from the next grade level though, as Kathy Richardson notes it is important to go deeper with concepts rather than to jump to the next ones.
A student can be an emergent learner in one area and an advanced fluent learner in another. We shouldn't give students labels that stick with them all year. As Dr. Kim Reid always said, "Labels are for boxes." Although we need a way to describe how students are doing in particular areas, we must never categorize them with fixed labels. "Rather than viewing some children as 'low' or 'behind' or 'lacking in skills,' kidwatching teachers view all children as creative, capable learners – on their way to 'achieving control over the conventions of [math]- always "in process" always moving forward . . . ' (Flukey, 1997, p. 219 cited in Owocki & Goodman, 2002)." Students move and develop along their own trajectory. With the appropriate scaffolding we can teach everybody and move them to achieving grade level standards.			

Rotations

Teachers can assign students where they are going to go, visiting different stations every day. Another way to do it is to give the student a menu for the week with Can Do's and Must Do's. Either way, students should do fluency, word problems, place value and work from the current unit of study.

Standards-Based

Every guided math lesson should be centered around priority/readiness standards. There are so many standards to teach, so we have to focus. We have to get in there, dig deep and discuss ideas so that students can learn them. When students sit down in the group, the first thing the teacher should talk about is the work they are going to be doing for the day. The *I can* or *I am* learning to statement should be up, and the students should discuss what they are going to be learning and what the criteria of success for that learning will look like. There is an ongoing discussion about whether to say *I can* or *I am* learning to. *I can* is more of a statement about what students will be able to do in the future. *I am* learning to speaks more to the continuum of learning and allows for students to be at different places along that continuum.

Dixon points out that, sometimes, we shouldn't tell the students the *I can* statement at the beginning all of the time because then you are in essence tell the ending of the story before it begins (2018a). This is an excellent point; it depends on where you are at in the concept and skill cycle and what the lesson of the day is. If you are trying to get students to explore and wonder about something, then don't upfront it, but discuss it at the end after they have explored the topic. However, if you are working on something that you have been doing for a while, you can say, "Today we are going to continue looking at . . . "

Depth of Knowledge

Guided math lessons are about building Depth of Knowledge with students. They should reach a variety of levels, not just level one activities. For example, instead of just telling stories like: There were 3 boxes with 4 cupcakes in each box. How many cupcakes are there? Teachers should ask questions like: The answer is 12 cupcakes. What is the question? Instead of just asking what is 3×2 teachers should also say things like give me two different ways to make 15. We want students to be reasoning about numbers in a variety of ways, using as many scaffolds as they need to become confident and competent.

Scaffolding

Scaffolds are a fundamental part of guided math lessons. There are so many different types of scaffolds. We are going to discuss grouping scaffolds, language scaffolds and tool scaffolds. Grouping scaffolds help students to become proficient by having students work with partners and in small groups, before they practice the skill on their own. This is the social aspect of grappling with the content. Oftentimes, students learn a great deal from each other through discussions and interactions. In the group, you can partner the students up and watch them play the game, take notes and ask different questions to guide them as they work together.

Language is often scaffolded with illustrated pictures of the vocabulary and language stems on sentence strips. Dixon (2018b) talks about how in the beginning of learning about a concept that it can be productive for students to have to explain the topic without the "cover" of the vocabulary. Meaning that sometimes students will use words but not understand the concepts, but their lack of understanding can be hidden by the use of the correct vocabulary. If they don't have that, then they have to explain the math. In later lessons, when students understand the math, then it's ok to upfront the vocabulary.

Scaffolding is so important and yet we have to be really careful not to overscaffold and as Dixon warns to also avoid "just in case" scaffolding (2018c). We want to help students as they need it, but we do not want to steal the struggle. Students need the opportunity to engage in the productive struggle, but it should not be an unproductive struggle (Hiebert & Grouws, 2007; Blackburn, 2018). There is a very careful balance act that teachers conduct when scaffolding in a guided math group.

In the guided math group, teachers should make sure that tools are part of the learning cycle. In planning to unpack the concepts and skills in small groups, teachers should think about the ways in which students can wrestle with topics concretely, pictorially and abstractly. There should also be an emphasis on verbalization and contextualization (NCTM, 2014). The magic of the manipulatives is the conversation and the activities that are done along with them. Students need to reflect on and explain the concepts and how the manipulatives are being used to model those concepts. In a small group, students should be doing the math and exploring and discussing the ideas as they use the manipulatives (Ball, 1992; Baroody, 1989; Bruner, 1960; Burns, n.d.)

Engagement

Engagement is important. Research links engagement to students' *affect*—their feelings and emotions about learning (Mcleod, 1992 cited in Ingram). We find that students' engagement is shaped around the sociocultural environment in which they are learning: how they are constructing knowledge together through discussions, activities and the norms of learning (Op 't Eynde, 2004; Boaler & Greeno, 2000; Greeno, Collins, & Resnick, 1996). The interactions that students have in small guided math groups are very important. They help to shape students' mathematical identities—who and what they see themselves as in terms of a mathematician.

We find that students are engaged when they participate in strong lessons in a strong community. A strong lesson has a clear purpose, is relevant and makes sense to their lives; it is brain-friendly and flows easily allowing them to quickly get into a "good 'work-flow,'" dive deep into the material (Claflin, 2014). The strong community of learners in essence means that "they got each other's back!" Everybody is in it to win it with each other. Students are helpful, trusting, risk-taking and comfortable. In the small group, they should be willing to try things out and assured that it is not always going to work the first time and that they might not get it even the second time around but that with perseverance they can learn it.

Another really important aspect of working with children is the wonder of learning. The guided math table is a special experience. I like to have guided math journals and special pencils and toolkits for students to work with at the table. Students look forward to coming to the guided math group. Often, I use dice, dominos, cards and board games. Since the same structure can be used, the students are ready to work on the content. Meaning, if we play bingo, then students know that structure, so they can immediately focus on the content. I might play a divide by 1 bingo game with one group and a mixed facts division bingo game with another group.

Student Accountability

While the students are working in math workstations, they should be filling out different sheets of the work they are doing (see Figures 2.5, 2.6 and 2.7). They should be recording what they are doing. Some sheets record everything that students are doing. Other games, have students record only some of their work. The most important thing about math workshop is that you organize it well from the beginning. You must do the first 20 days. In the first 20 days you teach the students how to work in the workshop. Here is a resource for that: www.drnickinewton.com/downloads/

Students have to learn how to work independently before you start pulling them in to guided math groups. The premise of Math Workshop is that all students can work on their own productively, before you start working with them in small groups.

There are two key elements to a good workstation. The first is a clear goal for the workstation. Students need to know what the math is and how they are going to work on that math and what it looks like when they are actually learning that math. The second is that they have an accountability system so that they know the teacher will be monitoring their work.

Figure 2.5 Example 1: Student Recording Sheet

Comparing Numbers Roll the dice. Record your roll as a decimal. Compare with the symbols. Whoever has the highest number wins a point. Whoever gets 5 points first wins the round. Whoever wins 3 rounds wins the game.		
Partner 1	< = >	Partner 2

Figure 2.6 Example 2: Student Recording Sheet

Recording Sheet: Top It

I had 7 /8. My partner had 4/ 4 which made 1 whole. My partner had more than I did.

_____ is greater than _____.

_____ is less than _____.

_____ is the same as _____.

Figure 2.7 Example 3: Student Recording Sheet

Recording Sheet: Board Game

When I went around the board I solved several multiplication facts problems. I used different strategies to help me.

I solved:
$2 \times 2 = 4$
$3 \times 5 = 15$
$4 \times 6 = 24$

Key Points

♦ Assessment
♦ Grouping
♦ Differentiation
♦ Rotations
♦ Standards-based
♦ Depth of Knowledge
♦ Scaffolding
♦ Engagement
♦ Student accountability

Chapter Summary

The key to great guided math groups is assessment. When you have great assessments, then you can group appropriately for differentiation that matters. Lessons should be standards-based. Teachers must always plan for the level of rigor in the lesson. Lessons should be scaffolded with language supports, tools, templates and student grouping. All the other students must be accountable to the work they are doing in the workstations. Engagement is necessary.

Reflection Questions

1. What specific assessments do you have around the priority standards?
2. In what ways are you evaluating your lessons for rigor?
3. In what ways are you scaffolding lessons?
4. How do you know that the other students are on task and learning in the math workstation?

References

Ball, D. L. (1992). Magical hopes: Manipulatives and the reform of math education. *American Educator: The Professional Journal of the American Federation of Teachers, 16*(2), 14–18, 46–47.

Baroody, A. J. (1989). Manipulatives don't come with guarantees. *Arithmetic Teacher, 37*(2), 4–5.

Blackburn, B. (2018). Retrieved January 5, 2020 from www.ascd.org/ascd-express/vol14/num11/productive-struggle-is-a-learners-sweet-spot.aspx

Boaler, J., & Greeno, J. G. (2000). Identity, agency, and knowing in mathematical worlds. In J. Boaler (Ed.), *Multiple perspectives on mathematics teaching and learning* (pp. 171–200). Westport, CT: Ablex Publishing.

Bruner, J. S. (1960). On learning mathematics. *The Mathematics Teacher, 53*(8), 610–619.

Burns, M. (n.d.). *How to make the most of manipulatives*. Retrieved August 28, 2016 from http://teacher.scholastic.com/lessonrepro/lessonplans/instructor/burns.htm?nt_id=4&url=http://store.scholastic.com/Books/Hardcovers/Harry-Potter-and-the-Chamber-of-SecretsThe-Illustrated-Edition-Book-2?eml=SSO/aff/20160429/21181/banner/EE/affiliate/////2-247765/&affiliate_id=21181&click_id=1707726852

Claflin, P. (2014). Retrieved January 20, 2020 from www.theanswerisyes.org/2014/12/08/student-engagement-checklist/

Dixon. (2018a). Retrieved January 4, 2020 from www.dnamath.com/blog-post/five-ways-we-undermine-efforts-to-increase-student-achievement-and-what-to-do-about-it/

Dixon. (2018b). Retrieved January 4, 2020 from www.dnamath.com/blog-post/five-ways-we-undermine-efforts-to-increase-student-achievement-and-what-to-do-about-it-part-4-of-5/

Dixon. (2018c). Retrieved January 4, 2020 from www.dnamath.com/blog-post/five-ways-we-undermine-efforts-to-increase-student-achievement-and-what-to-do-about-it-part-3-of-5/

Greeno, J. G., Collins, A. M., & Resnick, L. B. (1996). Cognition and learning. In D. C. Berliner & R. C. Calfee (Eds.), *Handbook of educational psychology* (pp. 15–46). London: Prentice Hall International.

Hiebert, J., & Grouws, D. A. (2007). The effects of classroom mathematics teaching on students' learning. In F. K. Lester Jr. (Ed.), *Second handbook of research on mathematics teaching and learning* (pp. 371–404). Charlotte, NC: Information Age.

McLeod, D. B. (1992). Research on affect in mathematics education: A reconceptualization. In D. Grouws (Ed.), *Handbook of research on mathematics teaching and learning* (pp. 575–596). New York: NCTM and Macmillan.

National Council of Teachers of Mathematics. (2014). *Principles to actions: Ensuring mathematical success for all*. Reston, VA: National Council of Teachers of Mathematics.

Op 't Eynde, P. (2004). A socio-constructivist perspective on the study of affect in mathematics education. In M. J. Hoines & A. B. Fuglestad (Eds.), *28th conference of the international group for the psychology of mathematics education* (Vol. 1, pp. 118–122). Bergen, Norway: Bergen University College.

Owocki, G., & Goodman, Y. M. (2002). *Kidwatching: Documenting children's literacy development*. Portsmouth, NH: Heinemann.

Richardson, K. (n.d.). Retrieved January 17, 2020 from http://assessingmathconcepts.com/

Shafer, L. (2016). *Summer math loss. Why kids lose math knowledge, and how families can work to counteract it*. Retrieved January 15, 2019 from www.gse.harvard.edu/news/uk/16/06/summer-math-loss

3

Architecture of a Small Group Lesson

Guided math groups can look many different ways. Sometimes they are more of an exploration of a concept with manipulatives like ten frames and counters; other times they are practicing a skill in the form of a dice game. The elements of the guided math lesson are the same, but the sequencing can be different. For example, you might start with an energizer and then review a skill and play a game to practice that skill. On the other hand, you might be exploring multiplication of a number with Cuisenaire rods first and then afterwards discuss what the math you were exploring was about.

Oftentimes a small group lesson should begin with an introduction to the lesson. In this introduction, students will often go over the agenda. The teacher should usually write it up as an agenda so students know what the general outline of the lesson is and what they will be doing. At some point in the lesson, depending on the type of lesson, the teacher would then go over the "*I am* learning to" statement as well as what it looks like when students can actually do that skill or understand that concept.

After that is discussed, everyone should talk about the math vocabulary and phrases that are associated with the current topic, if they are already familiar with the words. This is very important because everyone will use this vocabulary throughout the lesson. However, sometimes the vocabulary is discussed at the end of the lesson (see Dixon, 2018). In this case, the students talk about what they were doing and name it with math words.

Then, the lesson begins with either a discussion, an exploration or an activity. The teacher might model it or might just jump into the topic. Oftentimes, the teacher will ask the students to give their input about the topic before they begin. After a time of exploration, the students will begin to further explore the topic, either on their own, with a partner or with the whole small group.

At the end, the teacher will lead the debrief. This is where the students will discuss what the math was for the day, as well as how they practiced that math. They should also talk about how they feel they are doing with that math. This is the part of the lesson where students are reflecting and monitoring their process. They talk about the parts of the topic that are "easy-peasy" and the parts that are "tricky." Language is important, so instead of saying difficult or hard, I tend to say "tricky, fuzzy or climbing." Using a mountain metaphor can help students explain their journey. I explain to students that they could be just looking at the mountain from the base, climbing but not at the top yet, almost at the top or at the top (whereby they can say *it's sunny on the summit*).

Planning

Planning is key (see Figures 3.1 through 3.6). As you are planning for the guided math lesson, it is important to think about the differences between the content, the context and the activity. The content could be to teach students how to compare fractions in a variety of ways. The context could be a story about where students have to compare fractions. The activity could be to play a

    DOI: 10.4324/9781003169581-3

card game where they have to compare fractions. This comes up when mapping math content. There is a difference between an activity and a skill. An activity is to actually do something, like play a doubles board game. The skill is the verb—to be able to double a number. The teacher should be planning success criteria for both the product and the process. An example of the content criteria:

I am going to *play a multiplication game.*
So that I can practice *multiplying 2 digit numbers by 2 digit numbers.*
I will know that I can do it when I can use a variety of strategies and models.

An example of process criteria is to think about what practices you want students to be able to do:

♦ I can *explain* how to multiply 2-digit numbers with different strategies.
♦ I can *model* multiplying 2-digit numbers.

Clarke states that when we define process success criteria for students, it helps them do these six things:

1. Ensure appropriate focus
2. Provide opportunity to clarify their understanding
3. Identify success for themselves
4. Begin to identify where the difficulties lie
5. Discuss how they will improve
6. Monitor their own progress

(cited in Dyer, n.d.)

In the guided math group, everyone should know what the criteria is and should discuss it. Dyer notes that it is important for students to think about the "How will we know? question. When students wrestle with this question they begin "to understand the learning behind the learning target."

> This enables students to better understand what teachers expect them to know, understand, or be able to do, as well as what constitutes a proficient performance. This allows students to support each other and take responsibility for their own learning by helping them accurately and appropriately evaluate learning against shared expectations and make any necessary adjustments to the learning. Students become activated as learners.
>
> (Dyer, n.d.)

Think about this in terms of your guided math lessons. Do the students understand the success criteria? Do they know what they are expected to know, understand and be able to do? What are you looking for in the products or performances to know that the students were successful? How will you judge if it was successful? What will you use to judge the effectiveness of the product or performance? What counts as successful?

If the objective is for students to learn different efficient and flexible strategies for adding, then the success criteria might be that:

♦ Students' explanations include the names of the strategies
♦ Students can discuss different ways to think about the same problem
♦ In the explanations, students include a clear description of what they did (they can verbalize the strategy)
♦ Students can model their thinking

You could also have this discussion at the end of the lesson, after students have explored many different strategies. You could then talk about what it means to be flexible and efficient. You could have a checklist or rubric that has the criteria on it.

In the guided math group, the goal is for both teacher and students to be questioning. The expected answers should require thinking, not just a quick yes or no. Students should be thinking and explaining the work. Guided math should not be show and tell. It should be teachers springboarding students into mathematical thinking. The guided math group is a space for the "having of a very good idea" by all. In the guided math group the students should be taking the responsibility for learning and reflecting on their learning, as well as evaluating themselves and others. They should not be passive listeners or just "yes men and women." They should be active participants in the construction of rich mathematical ideas. To make this happen, there must be a great deal of planning.

Planning Templates

In the guided math group, there can be an agenda. Whether or not you make it public, the teacher should have an idea of the structure of the lesson. I usually make it public.

Introduction

Agenda

♦ *I am* learning to/*I can*
♦ Vocabulary/language frames
♦ Launch by teacher
♦ Student activity (alone/pairs/group)
♦ Wrap-up/reflection
♦ Next steps

Planning and Preparation

In order for teachers to be able to springboard students into mathematical thinking, they have to know what they want students to gain in the small group lesson, what all the elements needed in each lesson are, what the next steps are and what the expectations are at each level in order to move students forward in their understanding. There are many different planning templates, but they basically all have the same information. When planning it is important to think about the big idea, the enduring understanding, the essential question, the *I am* learning to statement, the assessments and possibly on the same template or a different one, the workstations or menu activities. The following templates can be used individually or together at different times to clearly lay out the plan and will allow the teacher to have a clear detailed map of what is happening and where they want students to go next. See the list of the templates below (see Figures 3.1–3.9).

Figure 3.1 Quick Plan

Week	Assessments	Workstations
Big Idea:	Entrance Slips:	Group 1
Enduring Understanding:	Exit Slips:	Group 2
Essential Question		Group 3
I am learning to….		Group 4

Figure 3.2 Guided Math Planning Template 1

Unit of Study: Big Idea: Enduring Understanding: Standard:			Essential Question: Vocabulary: Language Frame: I Can Statement:	
	Group 1:	Group 2:	Group 3:	Group 4:
Monday	Lesson: Materials: DOK Level: Concrete/Pictorial/ Abstract	Lesson: Materials: DOK Level: Concrete/Pictorial/ Abstract	Lesson: Materials: DOK Level: Concrete/Pictorial/ Abstract	Lesson: Materials: DOK Level: Concrete/Pictorial/ Abstract
Tuesday	Lesson: Materials: DOK Level: Concrete/Pictorial/ Abstract	Lesson: Materials: DOK Level: Concrete/Pictorial/ Abstract	Lesson: Materials: DOK Level: Concrete/Pictorial/ Abstract	Lesson: Materials: DOK Level: Concrete/Pictorial/ Abstract
Wednesday	Lesson: Materials: DOK Level: Concrete/Pictorial/ Abstract	Lesson: Materials: DOK Level: Concrete/Pictorial/ Abstract	Lesson: Materials: DOK Level: Concrete/Pictorial/ Abstract	Lesson: Materials: DOK Level: Concrete/Pictorial/ Abstract
Thursday	Lesson: Materials: DOK Level: Concrete/Pictorial/ Abstract	Lesson: Materials: DOK Level: Concrete/Pictorial/ Abstract	Lesson: Materials: DOK Level: Concrete/Pictorial/ Abstract	Lesson: Materials: DOK Level: Concrete/Pictorial/ Abstract
Friday	Lesson: Materials: DOK Level: Concrete/Pictorial/ Abstract	Lesson: Materials: DOK Level: Concrete/Pictorial/ Abstract	Lesson: Materials: DOK Level: Concrete/Pictorial/ Abstract	Lesson: Materials: DOK Level: Concrete/Pictorial/ Abstract

Figure 3.3 Guided Math Planning Template 2

Guided Math Groups	
Big Ideas: Enduring Understandings: Essential Questions: Vocabulary: Language Frames:	Cycle of Engagement: Concrete, Pictorial, Abstract Depth of Knowledge Level: 1 2 3 4 Standard/I can statement:
Group 1: Novice Students:	Group 2: Apprentice Students:
Group 3: Practitioner Students:	Group 4: Expert Students:

Figure 3.4 Guided Math Planning Template 3

Guided Math Lesson Plan: Group:		
Week: Big Idea: Enduring Understanding:	Standard: I can/I am learning to statement:	Vocabulary: Language Frame: Materials:
Lesson: Intro: Guided Practice: Individual Practice: Sharing: Debrief:		
Comments/Notes: Next Steps:		

Figure 3.5 Guided Math Planning Template 4

Guided Math Lesson		
Big Ideas: Enduring Understandings: Essential Questions:	Vocabulary: Language Frame:	Standard: I can/I am learning to…. Concrete/Pictorial/Abstract
Dok Level: 1 2 3 4	Goal: ♦ Remediate ♦ Teach ♦ Dive Deeper	Materials/Tools <table><tr><td>dice</td><td>board games</td><td>unifix cubes/bears/tiles</td></tr><tr><td>dominos</td><td>counters</td><td>base ten blocks</td></tr><tr><td>deck of cards</td><td>calculators</td><td>pattern blocks</td></tr><tr><td>white boards/ markers</td><td>gm journals</td><td>geoboards</td></tr></table>
Beginning of the Lesson	Guided Practice	Independent Practice
Assessment/Exit Slip	Discussion	Questions
Comments/Notes: Ahas: Wow: Rethink: Next Moves:		

Figure 3.6 Guided Math Planning Template 5

Guided Math		
Group: Week:		
Big Idea: Enduring Understandings: Essential Questions:	Vocabulary: Language Frame: Dok Level: 1 2 3 4	Lessons: 1st 2nd 3rd
Content Questions:		
Name	What I noticed	Next Steps

Figure 3.7 Guided Math Planning Template 6

Topic:	
Big Idea: **Enduring Understanding:** **Essential Question:** I can statement:	Materials
Cycle of Engagement Concrete: Pictorial: Abstract	**Vocabulary & Language Frames** Vocabulary: Talk Frame:
	Other notes;

Figure 3.8 Differentiation

3 Differentiated Lessons		
Emerging	On Grade Level	Above Grade Level

WATCH OUT   Misunderstandings and Misconceptions

Figure 3.9 Guided Math Planning Sheet

Guided Math Planning Sheet	
Launch	
Model	
Checking for Understanding	
Guided Practice/ Checking for Understanding	
Set up for Independent Practice	

Key Points

♦ Architecture of the lesson
♦ *I am* learning to/*I can*
♦ Vocabulary/language frames
♦ Launch by teacher
♦ Student activity (alone/pairs/group)
♦ Wrap-up
♦ Next steps
♦ Planning template
♦ Discussion throughout

Chapter Summary

There are many different ways to do small guided math groups. Teachers must plan for the learning goal, the vocabulary supports, the tools, the launch of the lesson, the students practicing the math, the wrap-up, the reflection and the next steps. All of these elements are an important part of the lesson. They all contribute to the success of the guided math group. Using planning templates with these elements on them helps teachers to plan for each of the elements.

Questions

1. Do your guided math lessons have all of the elements in them?
2. What types of templates are you currently using for guided math groups?
3. What is an element that you need to focus on in the architecture?

References

Dixon, J. (2018). *Small Group Instruction {from the (Un)Productive Practices Series}*. Five Ways We Undermine Efforts to Increase Student Achievement (and what to do about it). Blog Post 4: www.dnamath.com/blog-post/five-ways-we-undermine-efforts-to-increase-student-achievement-and-what-to-do-about-it-part-4-of-5/

Dyer, K. (n.d.). Retrieved January 20, 2020 from www.nwea.org/blog/2018/what-you-need-to-know-when-establishing-success-criteria-in-the-classroom/

4

Talk in the Guided Math Group

One of the most important things that happen in the guided math group is the discussion. We have to teach students to be active participants and engaged listeners. We want them to respect each other deeply and seek to truly understand each other without judgement. They have to learn to develop and defend their thinking, justify their answers and respectfully disagree with each other. The National Council of Teachers of Mathematics (NCTM) defines math talk as "the ways of representing, thinking, talking, and agreeing and disagreeing that teachers and students use to engage in [mathematical] tasks" (NCTM, 1991).

Questions

It is so important to ask good questions. The questions should reach beyond the answer. As Phil Daro notes, we have to go "beyond answer-getting" (https://vimeo.com/79916037). The questions in the guided math group should be designed to get students to understand more fundamentally the mathematics of the grade level. Good questions don't just happen, they are planned for. The teacher should know ahead of time the types of questions that she will ask and why she will ask them. In the plan for the lesson, the teacher should brainstorm some possible questions that push student thinking. These are not yes or no questions, but rather ones that require students to explain themselves, show what they know and defend and justify their thinking (see Figure 4.1).

When students are sitting in that group, they should be having an engaging experience that builds mathematical knowledge and skills. At the table, students should be encouraged to actively participate. They should be thinking out loud, sharing their thoughts, respectively analyzing and critiquing the thoughts and actions of others and taking risks throughout the explorations. We should always be thinking about the levels of rigor of the conversation that the students are engaged in (see Figure 4.2).

It is very important to include *Open Questions* as part of your repertoire at the guided math table. Here is an example: *The answer is 2 with a remainder of 1. What is the question?* Although you will ask some questions that require students to remember a fact or show you that they can do a skill, your questions must extend beyond this level. You should be focusing on questions that have more than one answer or way of solving the problem.

Questions that Pique Curiosity

Your questions should pique curiosity. They should lead students into further explorations. They don't have to be answered immediately. Students should have a sense of wonder. There should be some "Aha" moments, some "Wow" moments and some "I don't get it" moments.

For example, "What if we didn't have addition?" "Tell me three situations in which you would use subtraction." "Why is multiplication important in real life?"

DOI: 10.4324/9781003169581-4

Figure 4.1 Planning for Great Questions

Before the Lesson	During the Lesson	After the Lesson
Plan what you want to get your students to think about. The tasks that we choose will determine the thinking that occurs.	**Observe, monitor and note what is happening in the group. Checklists, post-its and anecdotal note structures work well here.**	**Reflect, Assess, Decide what's next.**
How will you go about that? What questions will you ask them?	What is your data collection system during the lesson?	What did you see?
		What did you hear?
How will you set them up to actively listen and productively participate?	How will you scaffold student questioning?	What did the students do?
How will you get them to engage with the ideas of others?	How will you scaffold student to student interactions?	What do you need to do next?
		What instructional moves will you make?
How will you get them to offer detailed explanations of their own thinking using numbers, words and model?		What pedagogical moves will you make?
Plan for misconceptions. How will you address them and redirect students?		

Figure 4.2 Depth of Knowledge

Dok 1 Must Have.... At this level students are recalling information.	Dok 2 At this level students explain their thinking.	Dok 3 At this level students have to justify, defend and prove their thinking with objects, drawings and diagrams.
What is the answer to … ??? Can you model the problem? Can you identify the answer that matches this equation?	How do you know that the equation is correct? Can you pick the correct answer and explain why it is correct? How can you model that problem in more than one way? What is another way to model that problem? Can you model that on the ….??? Give me an example of a … type of problem…. Which answer is incorrect? Explain your thinking.	Can you prove that your answer is correct? Prove that… Explain why that is the answer… Show me how to solve that and explain what you are doing.

*Level 4 is more strategic project based thinking.

Student to Student Conversations

It is crucial that the teacher sets up a discussion where students are asking each other questions. They could have question rings, bookmarks, mini-anchor charts or other scaffolds to help them ask each other questions (see Figures 4.3–4.5). In these conversations one of the things that students are doing is listening to each other and comparing what they did.

Probing Questions

Teacher questions as well as student to student questions should provide insight into student thinking. During the guided math lesson and after it, the teacher should jot down what they have learned about student thinking, student knowledge and how they are making sense of the math they are learning.

Figure 4.3 Question Bookmark

Question Bookmark

Questions we could ask each other:

How do you know?

Are you sure about that?

What is another way to do that?

Why did you use that model?

Can you explain your thinking?

Figure 4.4 Talk Cards/Talk Ring

I agree because...	I disagree because..	I need some time to think.	Why is that true?
👍	👎	⏱	☑

Are you sure?	Do you agree or disagree?	Can you think of another way?	I'm confused still..
Yes I'm sure because No, I'm not sure. I'm thinking about it.	✓ or ✗	Way 1 Way 2	?

Figure 4.5 5 Talk Moves Poster

5 talk moves poster				
Revoice	Restate	Reason	Wait Time	Group participation
I heard you say…	*Who can say what she said in your own words?*	*Are you sure? Can you prove it?*	*Give me a few seconds*	*Who wants to add to that?*

Source: Adapted from Chapin, O'Connor, and Anderson (2009).

Scaffolding Questions for ELLs

Students should understand the questions being asked. The language should be accessible, and everyone should have a way to enter the conversation. When thinking about instruction with English Language Learners, we must consider the type of language support they will need (https://mathsolutions.com/math-talk/; http://fspsscience.pbworks.com/w/file/fetch/80214878/Leveled_20Questions_20for_20ELLs; www.aworldoflanguagelearners.com/asking-answering-questions-with-ells/). Oftentimes, they will need help with syntax and sentence structure, so it is important to scaffold these into the conversation. Give students an opportunity to refer to language stems, use language bookmarks, write down and/or draw the answer (see Figure 4.6).

Figure 4.6 Levels of Support

Low Levels of Support: (advanced language learners) (levels 3 & 4)	Moderate Levels of Support: (developing language learners) (level 2)	High Levels of Support: (emerging language learners) (level 1)
Use a word bank (illustrated)	Use a sentence frame	Allow students to draw/ write the answer
Explain how s/he did that?	I got the answer by _____.	Point to the….
Explain your thinking?	How can you use ____ to help you solve _____?	Show me your answer …
Explain your model/ strategy?	How can you model that?	Which is the best answer?
What are 2 ways you could model your thinking?	What is the name of that strategy? (mini-anchor chart)	What is the name of that strategy? Do you see it here? (mini-anchor chart of strategies)
Can you describe your thinking?	How did you do that?	Give students a model sentence and a sentence frame.
Can you show us what you did?	Why did you use that model/strategy?	How did you get the answer?
Can you describe how you did it?	How did s/he do that?	How did you _____?
Can you explain what s/he did?	Is it this or that?	Do you agree? Yes or no?
Why is that true?	Which strategy did you use? (visual support)	Show me the _____
Why is that not true?		Point to the _____
Explain how you did it.		Circle the ____
Decide if s/he is correct?		Can you point to the strategy you used?

Source: Adapted from http://fspsscience.pbworks.com/w/file/fetch/80214878/Leveled_20Questions_20for_20ELLswww.aworldoflanguagelearners.com/asking-answering-questions-with-ells/

Although these are structures for ELLs, they are great question types to consider with the various students you are working with. They are also great ways to think about scaffolding questions for special education students.

5 Talk Moves and More

The idea of having a framework for how students engage with each other is very important. Chapin et al. (2009) theorized this framework around 5 Talk Moves: revoicing, restating, wait time, group participation and reasoning. There are also other really helpful frameworks (Kazem & Hintz, 2014; O'Connell & O'Connor, 2007). In the section that follows we will explore how some of these can help us structure the discussions in guided math groups. Oftentimes, these structures are used together; for example, a teacher might ask someone to restate what someone said and then encourage the group to add on (see Figures 4.7 to 4.16).

Figure 4.7 Revoicing

Revoicing		
What it is...	**What it does**	**What it sounds like**
The teacher restates in the words of the student what they just said	This allows the student to hear back what they said, the other students to hear and process what has been said and everyone to think about it and make sure they understand it. This teaches students the power of hearing what they have said and trying to make sense of it.	*So you said… Is that correct?* *Let me make sure I understand, you are saying….* *So first you… and then you…* *So you used this model?* *So you used this strategy?*

Figure 4.8 Restating

Restating		
What it is...	**What it does**	**What it sounds like**
The teacher or other students restate in their own words what has been said. Then, they verify that restating with the original student.	This allows the student to hear back what they said, the other students to hear and process what has been said and everyone to think about it and make sure they understand it. This requires that students listen and pay attention to each other so they can restate what has been said. This teaches students how to listen to each other and make sense of what their peers are saying.	*Who can restate what Susie just said?* *Who can tell in their own words what Jamal just said?* *Who can explain what Carol meant when she said....?*

Figure 4.9 Wait Time

Wait Time		
What it is...	**What it does**	**What it sounds like**
Teachers and students give each other 20 – 30 seconds of uninterrupted time to think, write or draw about what they are doing. This is done after the question is asked and then also when the answer is given. Students should be given the time to think about the answer and then respond to it.	This allows students the time to gather their thoughts, clarify their thinking for themselves and just time to think. It gives more people time to process what is happening. It teaches them the power of stopping to think instead of rushing into a conversation.	*Ok, now I am going to ask some questions but I want you to take some think time before you answer.* *Terri, just gave an answer. Let's think about what she just said before we respond.* *Show me with a silent hand signal when you are ready.* *Let's give everyone some time to think about this...* *Is everybody ready to share or do you need more time....show me with a hand signal....*

Figure 4.10 Reasoning

Reasoning		
What it is...	**What it does**	**What it sounds like**
Teachers and students are asking each other for evidence and proof to defend and justify what they are saying.	This requires students to engage with each other's thinking. They must compare, contrast, justify and defend their thinking with the other group members. This teaches students the power of defending and justifying their thinking with evidence and proof.	*Why did you do that?* *Is that true?* *Why did you use that strategy?* *Can you prove it?* *Are you sure?* *How do you know?* *Why did you use that model?* *Does that make sense?* *Do you agree or disagree, and why or why not?* *How is your thinking like Tom's?* *Is there another way?*

Figure 4.11 Group Participation

Group participation		
What it is...	**What it does**	**What it sounds like**
Students write down or model their thinking and then share it with the whole group.	This allows students to focus on their own strategies and models, jot them down and then share them. This teaches students the power of justifying and defending their thinking.	*Use a model to show....* *Illustrate your strategy.* *On your white boards, show us...* *In your guided math journal, show your thinking with numbers, words or pictures... be ready to share it with the group...*

Figure 4.12 Making Connections

To make connections		
What it is...	**What it does**	**What it sounds like**
Teachers and students are asking each other to make connections with what has been said at the table.	It requires students to listen to each other and think about how what they did connects to what someone else did. This teaches students the power of making connections with each other's thinking.	*How is that the same as what Marta did?* *How is that different from what Joe did?* *This is like what Trini did...* *How are these models the same and how are they different?* *How are these strategies the same and how are they different?*

Figure 4.13 Partner Talk

Partner Talk		
What it is...	**What it does**	**What it sounds like**
Students talk with their math partners about the math before they share out with the group. They might even draw or write something to share out.	This allows students to think out the math with each other, try to make sense of it and then be able to explain it to the whole group. This teaches students the power of working together to make sense of the math.	*Turn and talk to your partner.* *Tell your partner what you think and why you think that.* *Show and explain to your partner what you did.* *Defend your thinking to your partner.*

Figure 4.14 Prompting for Student Participation

What it is	What it does	What it sounds like
The teacher or the students encourage each other to participate in the conversation.	This allows students to participate with each other in the discussion. It openly asks for participation that builds on what has just been said. This teaches students the power of participating in a discussion.	*Who would like to add to that?* *Who wants to say more?* *How is what you did the same or different from the way Hong did it?* *Is there another model?* *Is there another strategy?* *Is there another way?*

Figure 4.15 Clarifying One's Own Thinking

What it is...	What it does	What it sounds like
Teachers and students take the time to clarify their thinking.	It allows students to expand on their original thoughts. It requires them to give more examples, show more models and explain at a deeper level.	*Can you explain that further?* *Can you tell us more?* *What does that mean?* *Can you show us a model and explain it?* *Can you illustrate your strategy and explain it?*

Figure 4.16 Reflecting/Revising/Probing

Reflecting/Revising/Probing		
What it is...	**What it does**	**What it sounds like**
The teacher and the students take time to reflect on what has been said and possibly revise their thinking.	This gives students an opportunity to rethink about what they have just done. They get permission to change their minds. It teaches them the power of reflecting and revising their work.	*Did anybody change their mind?* *Did anybody revise their thinking?* *Now that you see this model, what do you think?* *Now that you see this strategy, what do you think now?* *Thinking about what Jamal just said, how does that help us with our thinking?*

It is very important to use different talk moves and structures with students during guided math group in order to scaffold the discussions. The preceding structures can definitely get you started doing this. It is important to plan for what you want to work on so that it isn't just random conversations. You should be explicit with students when teaching these structures. For example, you might say, "Today we are working on wait time. I want you to think about giving each other the time to think as we talk. Remember, just because you are ready, doesn't mean your neighbor is yet."

Key Points

♦ Questions matter
♦ Plan for great questions
♦ DOK questions
♦ Questions that pique curiosity
♦ Student to student conversations
♦ Scaffolding questions for ELLs
♦ 5 talk moves and more

Chapter Summary

Planning matters. We must plan for good conversations. We must think about the ways in which we want our students to engage with each other and then actively do that in our groups. Think about the level of rigor of our questions. Think about what kinds of questions pique curiosity.

Consider how we get students to engage with each other respectfully, confidently and competently. We must stay conscious of scaffolding our questions for ELLs so that everyone has a way to enter the conversations. We need to consider the different types of talk moves that allow us to have rigorous, engaging, and productive conversations.

Reflection Questions

1. What stands out for you in this chapter?
2. What will you enact right away?
3. What questions do you still have?

References

Chapin, S., O'Connor, C., & Anderson, N. (2009). *Classroom discussions: Using math talk to help students learn, Grades K-6* (2nd ed.). Sausalito, CA: Math Solutions Publications.

Daro, P. Retrieved December 11, 2020 from https://vimeo.com/79916037

Kazemi, E., & Hintz, A. (2014). *Intentional talk: How to structure and lead productive mathematical discussions*. Portland, ME: Steinhouse.

NCTM. (1991). *Professional standards for teaching mathematics*. Reston, VA: NCTM.

O'Connell, S., & O'Connor, K. (2007). *Introduction to communication, grades 3–5*. Heinemann.

Retrieved November 24, 2020 from http://fspsscience.pbworks.com/w/file/fetch/80214878/Leveled_20Questions_20for_20ELLs

Retrieved November 24, 2020 from https://mathsolutions.com/math-talk/

Retrieved November 24, 2020 from www.aworldoflanguagelearners.com/asking-answering-questions-with-ells/

5

Fluency

Fluency is a multi-dimensional concept. We like to think of it as a four-legged stool: accuracy, flexibility, efficiency and instant recall (Brownell & Chazal, 1935; Brownell, 1956/1987; Kilpatrick, Swafford, & Findell, 2001; National Council of Teachers of Mathematics, 2000). Although we eventually want students to have instant recall, we need them to understand what they are doing with the numbers first. The emphasis in the guided math group is to do a variety of engaging, interactive, rigorous and student-friendly activities that build a fundamental understanding of how numbers are in relationship with each other. As you explore the facts with the students, be sure to do concrete, pictorial and abstract activities with them. There should be several ways for students to practice that are fun and challenging. Students should keep track of how they are doing as well.

Basic fact fluency is a major part of third grade. Fourth grade students should come into the grade having fluency within 100 for multiplication and division and within 1000 for addition and subtraction. However, often times, these facts need to be reviewed and firmed up with special emphasis on learning higher addition and subtraction fact strategies, such as doubles, doubles plus 1 and 2, bridging ten and half facts. In fourth grade students continue with all four operations. With addition and subtraction, students work on fluency within 1 million using traditional strategies. With multiplication and division, they begin to work with multi-digit numbers. Research says that we should devote at least 10 minutes a day to fluency practice (NCEE, 2009). It should be done as energizers and routines, in workstations and sometimes as guided math lessons. Teachers should integrate fluency work throughout the year because students learn their basic facts at different times.

DOI: 10.4324/9781003169581-5

Research Note 🔍

- There has been a long debate on traditional fact-based instruction centered around memorization and strategy-based instruction centered around number sense and using strategies. Strategy-based instruction helps students to understand the math they are doing and to do it with eventual flexibility, efficiency, automaticity and accuracy (Baroody, Purpura, Eiland, Reid, & Paliwal, 2016; Henry & Brown, 2008; Thornton, 1978).
- Boaler (2015) argues that the emphasis of rote memorization through repetition and timed testing is "unnecessary and damaging."
- Several scholars have promoted engaging practice through strategy-based games, and activities can scaffold learning of basic facts (Van de Walle, 2007; Godfrey & Stone, 2013; Bay-Williams & Kling, 2019; Newton, 2016; Newton, Record, & Mello, 2020).

In this chapter, we will explore:

- Multiplicative comparison
- Division math mats
- Subtraction across zeroes
- Division of a double-digit number by a single-digit number

Overview

Figure 5.1 Overview

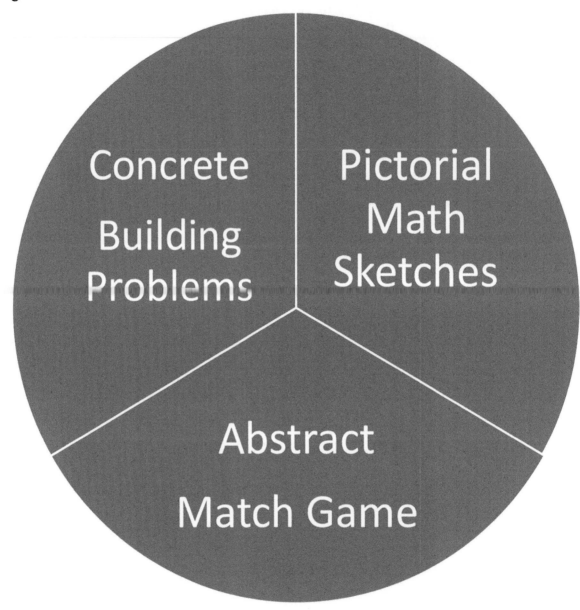

Figure 5.2 Planning Temp

Multiplicative Comparison Problems

Big Idea: Numbers, Operation Meanings & Relationships; Basic Facts & Algorithms **Enduring Understanding:** Students will understand multiplicative comparison problems where you are looking for the bigger part.	**Materials** ♦ Tools: counters (tiles, cubes, circles)
Essential Question: In what ways do we use multiplicative comparison in real life? Why is it important? **I can statement:** I can solve multiplicative comparison problems where you are looking for the bigger part.	**Vocabulary & Language Frames** **Vocabulary:** factors, array, product, compare, as many, as much **Math Talk:** _____ has _____ as many as _____.
Cycle of Engagement **Concrete:** 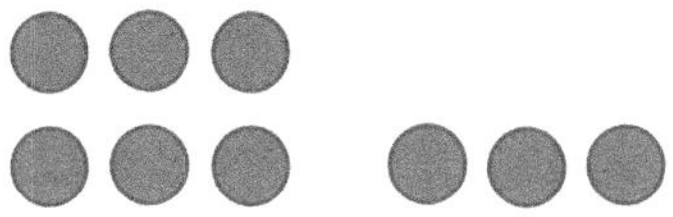 ⚪⚪⚪ ⚪⚪⚪ ⚪⚪⚪	**Math Processes/Practices** ♦ Problem Solving ♦ Reasoning ♦ Models ♦ Tools ♦ Precision ♦ Structure ♦ Pattern
Pictorial: 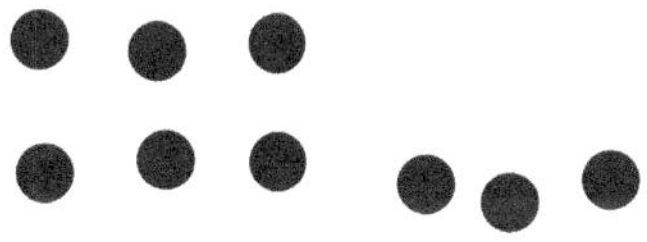 ● ● ● ● ● ● ●●●	**Abstract:** Katie has 3 rings. Monique has twice as many as she does. $3 \times 2 = 6$

Figure 5.3 Differentiation

3 Differentiated Lessons		
In this series of lessons, students are working on multiplicative comparison. They are developing this concept through concrete activities, pictorial activities and abstract activities. Here are some things to think about as you do these lessons.		
Emerging	**On Grade Level**	**Above Grade Level**
Do a lot of work with students building out the multiplicative comparison problems with manipulatives.	Do a lot of work with different manipulatives and having the students do math sketches.	Talk about different models.

 Looking for Misunderstandings and Common Errors

There are 3 different types of multiplicative comparison problems. Students are looking for either the bigger part, the smaller part or the difference. The difference is the hardest type of problem. Teachers should start these problems with small numbers and eventually work up to larger ones.

Figure 5.4 Anchor Chart

Multiplicative Comparison Problems

Build with concrete materials

Sketch

Abstract

Marissa has 2 marbles. Her sister has twice as many as she does. How many does her sister have?

$$2 \times 2 = 4$$

Concrete Lesson

Figure 5.5 Concrete Introduction

Introduction to Concrete Explorations

Launch	**Teacher:** Today we are going to work on multiplication problems where we are working on comparing. **Vocabulary:** compare, expression, equation, product, factor, two times as many **Math Talk:** _____ has _____ as many as _____
Model	**Teacher:** We are going to be looking at problems where we compare things. Listen to this problem: *Luke had 4 marbles. His brother had 2 times as many. How many did his brother have?* How might we solve this problem with our tiles? **Katie:** I did this. 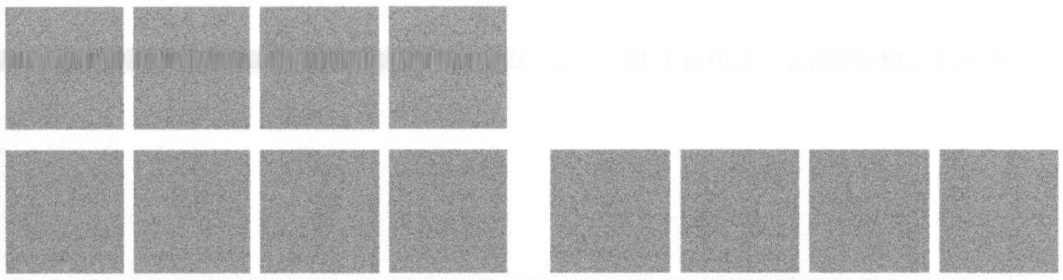
Checking for Understanding	**Teacher:** Who can explain what Katie did? **Demonte:** I can. She had 4 on top for Luke and then 2 times as many on the bottom. **Teacher:** Listen to the next one. *Maite had 3 rings. Her sister had twice as many as she did. How many did her sister have?* **Hong:** I can do it. There are 3 on top and then 3 on the bottom and then 3 more because there were twice as many. Maite's sister had 6. **Teacher:** Ok, so I am going to give each one of you a problem to solve. I want you to solve it any way you want and then explain it back to the group. Model it with your manipulatives.

Figure 5.6 Student Activity

	Concrete Student Activity
Guided Practice/ Checking for Understanding	**Teacher:** Who wants to go next? *Jay-Jay has 2 marbles. His brother has 3 times as many as he does. How many does his brother have?* **Bessie:** I can do it. There are 2 on top and then 2 three times on the bottom. Jay-Jay's brother had 6.
Set up for Independent Practice	Every child shares out their problem and how they solved it. We are going to be talking more about this in the upcoming days. Are there any questions? What was interesting today? What was tricky?

Figure 5.7 Lesson Close

Close
• What did we do today? • What was the math we were practicing? • Was this easy or tricky? • Turn to a partner and state one thing you learned today.

Visual Lesson

Figure 5.8 Visual Introduction

	Introduction to Visual Explorations
Launch	**Teacher:** Today we are going to work on multiplication problems where we are working on comparing. **Vocabulary**: compare, expression, equation, product, factor, two times as many **Math Talk:** _____ has _____ as many as _____
Model	**Teacher:** We are going to be looking at problems where we compare things. Today we are going to use math sketches to show our thinking. Listen to this problem: *Larry had 5 marbles. His brother had 2 times as many. How many did his brother have?* How might we solve this problem with math sketches? **Katie:** I did this. His brother has 10.
Checking for Understanding	**Teacher:** Listen to this problem: *Leti had 3 rings. Her sister had 3 times as many as she did. How many did her sister have?* **Vincent:** I did this. Her sister has 9 rings. **Teacher:** I am going to give each one of you a problem. I want you to tell us what you did and explain your thinking.

Figure 5.9 Student Activity

	Visual Student Activity
Guided Practice/ Checking for Understanding	**Teacher:** Listen to this problem: *Kyle had 3 toy trucks. His brother had 2 times as many as he did. How many did his brother have?* **Vicki:** I did this. His brother has 6 trucks. 2 times as many means you have to put what he had 2 times. 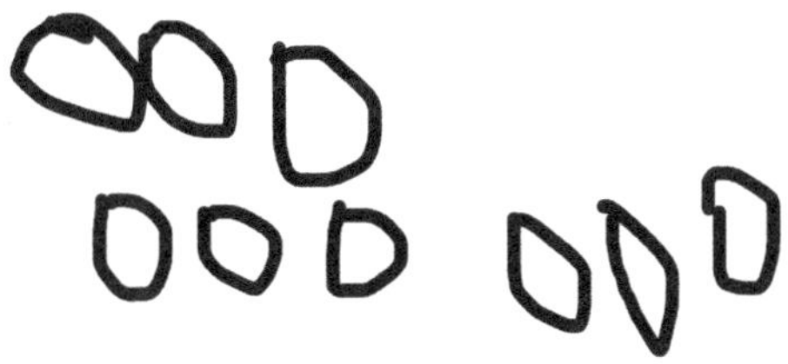 OOO OO OOO OOO
Set up for Independent Practice	*Teacher gives everybody a chance to do and discuss a problem. After everyone has shared the lesson ends.* We are going to be talking more about that in the upcoming days. Are there any questions? What was interesting today? What was tricky?

Figure 5.10 Lesson Close

Close
• What did we do today? • What was the math we were practicing? • What were we doing with our number wands? • Was this easy or tricky? • Turn to a partner and state one thing you learned today.

Abstract Lesson

Figure 5.11 Abstract Introduction

<table>
<tr><th colspan="2">Introduction to Abstract Explorations</th></tr>
<tr>
<td>Launch</td>
<td>

Teacher: Today we are going to work on multiplication problems where we are working on comparing.

Vocabulary: compare, expression, equation, product, factor, two times as many

Math Talk: _____ has _____ as many as _____

</td>
</tr>
<tr>
<td>Model</td>
<td>

Teacher: Today we are going to do a match activity. You are going to work with your partner to match cards that go together. Here is an example of the 4 cards that go together.

2 times as many as 2	2×2	4	●● ● ● ● ●

</td>
</tr>
<tr>
<td>Checking for Understanding</td>
<td>

Teacher: I am going to give you a baggie with the cards all mixed up and you and your partner will match them up.

</td>
</tr>
</table>

Figure 5.12 Student Activity

	Abstract Student Activity			
Guided Practice/ Checking for Understanding	**Teacher:** Maite and Carlos tell me about one of your matches. **Maite:** We found these. 3 times as many as 2 is 6.			
	3 times as many as 2	3 × 2	6	• • •• •• ••
Set up for Independent Practice	The students come up with the answers and explain what they did. Teacher explains that this activity will be one of the choices in the workstations and that they should talk through different strategies with their math buddies.			

Figure 5.13 Lesson Close

Close
• What did we do today?   • What was the math we were practicing?   • What were we doing with our number wands?   • Was this easy or tricky?   • Turn to a partner and state one thing you learned today.

Figure 5.14 Cards

2 times as many as 2	2 × 2	4	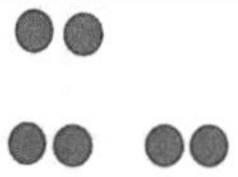 ●● ●● ●●
3 times as many as 3	3 × 3	9	 ●●● ●●● ●●● ●●●
2 times as many as 4	2 × 4	6	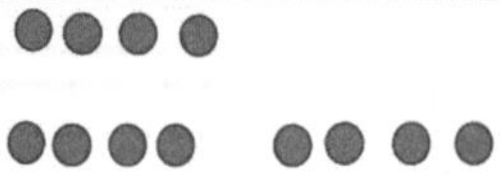 ●●●● ●●●● ●●●●
2 times as many as 1	2 × 1	6	 ● ●●
4 times as many as 2	3 × 2	6	 ●● ●● ●● ●● ●●
5 times as many as 2	3 × 2	6	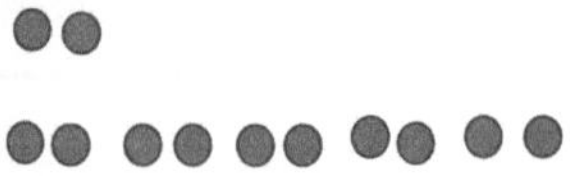 ●● ●● ●● ●● ●● ●●
4 times as many as 1	3 × 2	6	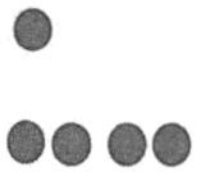 ● ●● ●●

Section Summary

Multiplicative comparison problems can be tricky for students. There are three types, and this one that we have looked at in this section tends to be the easiest for students. It is very important to spend some time building conceptual understanding by using the manipulatives and having the students build out the problem. Then they should move on to sketches. I also like to use centimeter paper and Cuisenaire ᵗᵐ rods when teaching this concept because I can go from the manipulative (which is the length of a centimeter) directly to modeling it on the centimeter paper so that we can easily lead into making bar/tape diagrams.

Overview

Figure 5.15 Overview

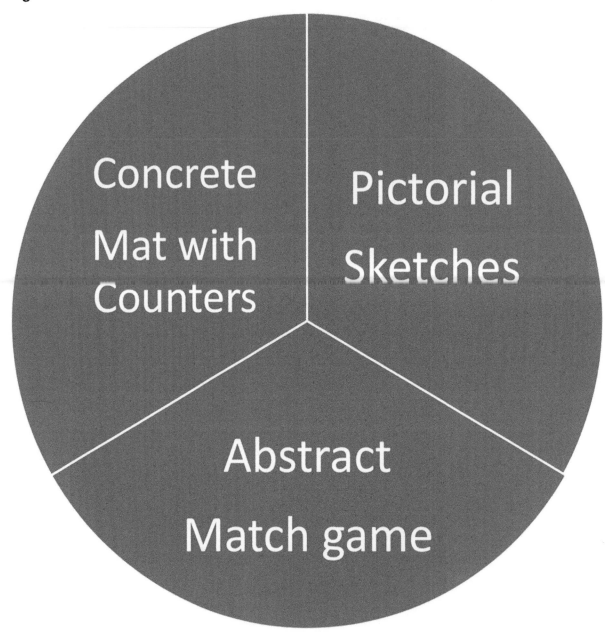

Figure 5.16 Planning Template

Division Mats	
Big Idea: Numbers, Operation Meanings & Relationships; Properties, Basic Facts & Algorithms **Enduring Understanding:** Students will understand that dividing can be sharing equally and that there can be leftovers/remainders. **Essential Question:** Why is division important? How do we use it in real life? **I can statement:** I can model division problems with a remainder. I can explain and defend my thinking.	**Materials** • Tools: counters (tiles, cubes, circles)
	Vocabulary & Language Frames **Vocabulary:** factors, array, product, quotient, divisor, dividend **Math Talk:** The quotient is _____. There is a remainder of _____.
Cycle of Engagement **Concrete:** $8 \div 4 = 2$ There is a remainder of 1. 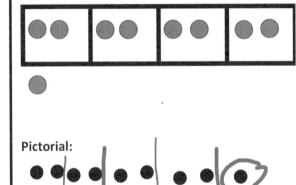 **Pictorial:**	**Math Processes/Practices** • **Problem Solving** • **Reasoning** • **Models** • **Tools** • **Precision** • **Structure** • **Pattern** **Abstract:** $9 \div 4 = 2\frac{1}{4}$ or $9 = 4 \times 2 + 1$

Figure 5.17 Differentiation

3 Differentiated Lessons
In this series of lessons, students are working on dividing and exploring remainders. They are developing this concept through concrete activities, pictorial activities and abstract activities. Here are some things to think about as you do these lessons.

Emerging	On Grade Level	Above Grade Level
Division is more challenging than multiplication. Review subtraction. Also, do a great deal of problems using small numbers so students can visualize the math.	Students should work on understanding concepts such as what happens when 0 is divided by a number, what happens when dividing by 1, 2, the number itself etc.	Expand the number range.

Looking for Misunderstandings and Common Errors

Students have trouble with division. It is important to use division math mats with them because it helps them to physically act out the story as it is being told. After they do that, then they can do sketches. After they do that, they can move on to tape/bar diagrams.

Figure 5.18 Anchor Chart

Modeling Division with remainders

Concrete: 7 ÷ 3

Pictorial:

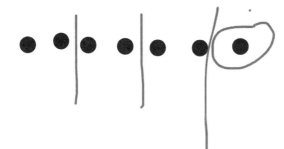

Abstract:

$$7 \div 3 = 2\tfrac{1}{3}$$
$$7 = 3 \times 2 + 1$$

Concrete Lesson

Figure 5.19 Introduction to Concrete Explorations

	Introduction
Launch	**Teacher:** Today we are going to work on division. **Vocabulary:** dividend, divisor, quotient, expression, equation. **Math Talk:** The quotient is _____. The dividend is ____. The divisor is ____.
Model	**Teacher:** We are going to be telling division stories. We will act them out on our mats. Who wants to go first? **Kay:** To solve this problem I gave each kid a donut and then there was one left over. So the answer is that each kid gets 1 donut and there is 1 leftover. **Donnie:** I will eat it! 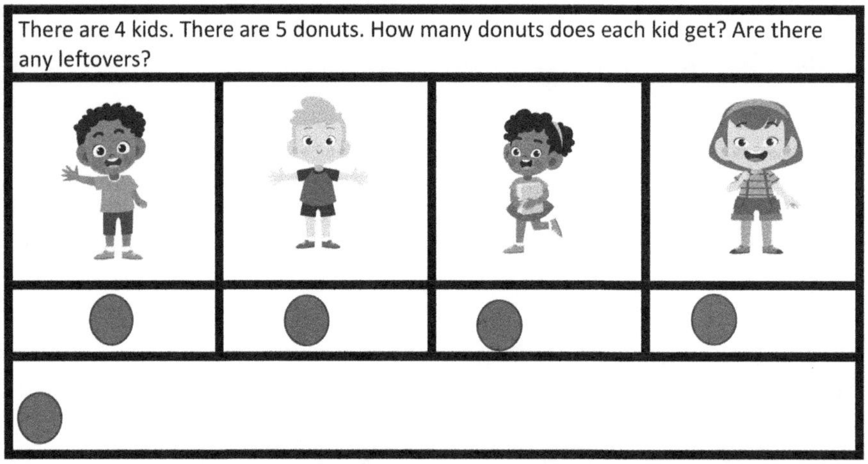

Checking for Understanding	**Teacher:** Who wants to go next? **Ray-Ray:** Each kid gets 2 donuts in this problem and 2 are left over. **Donnie:** I will eat them!  **Teacher:** Ok. I am going to give each one of you your own problem. I want you to read it. Solve it. Be ready to share how you did it. I am going to watch you and if you need help, look at our anchor charts, ask a math partner and of course you can ask me.

Figure 5.20 Student Activity

Guided Practice/ Checking for Understanding	The teacher reads 1 more that the students do together then they each get their own cards to work on. As they do their work, the teacher takes notes, asks questions and has a conversation with individual students. **Teacher:** Tell us about your problem Donnie. **Donnie:** Each kid gets 2 marbles and 1 is leftover. 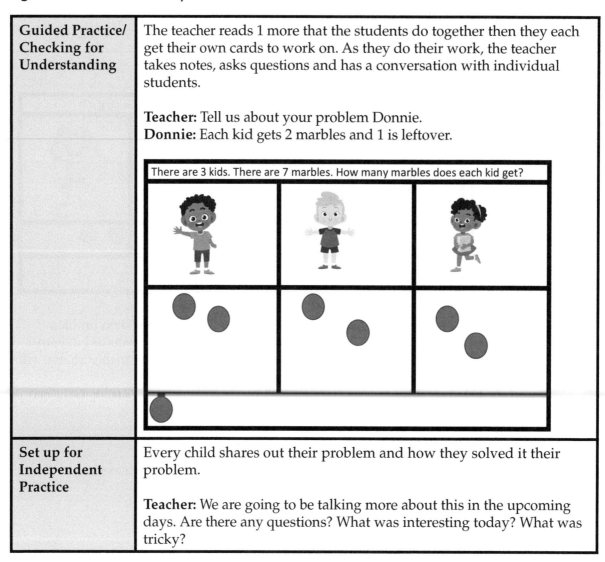
Set up for Independent Practice	Every child shares out their problem and how they solved it their problem. **Teacher:** We are going to be talking more about this in the upcoming days. Are there any questions? What was interesting today? What was tricky?

Figure 5.21 Lesson Close

Close
◆ What did we do today? ◆ What was the math we were practicing? ◆ What were we doing with our number wands? ◆ Was this easy or tricky? ◆ Turn to a partner and state one thing you learned today.

Figure 5.22 Division Mat Example Cards (Download)

Problem	

leftover

Equation:

There is a remainder of _____

Problem:

leftover

Equation:

There is a remainder of _____

Visual Lesson

Figure 5.23 Visual Introduction

Introduction to a Visual Explorations

Launch	**Teacher:** Today we are going to continue to work on division with remainders. **Vocabulary:** dividend, divisor, quotient, expression, equation **Math Talk:** The quotient is _____. The dividend is ____. The divisor is ____.
Model	**Teacher:** Today we are going do what we did yesterday, but today we are doing math sketches to solve our problems. Who wants to share their thinking first? **Tommy:** I did it. I got that each kid gets 1 donut and there is 1 leftover. 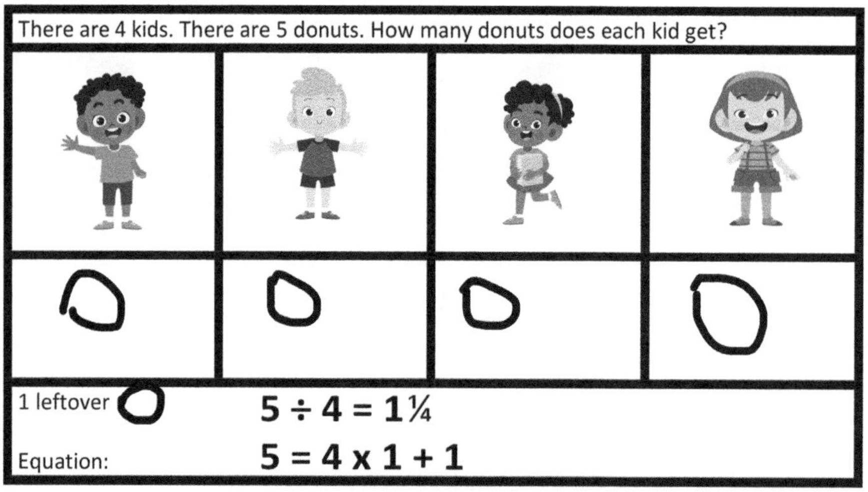 There are 4 kids. There are 5 donuts. How many donuts does each kid get? 1 leftover ○ $5 \div 4 = 1\frac{1}{4}$ Equation: $5 = 4 \times 1 + 1$
Checking for Understanding	Teacher: Ok. I am going to give each one of you your own problem. I want you to read it. Solve it. Be ready to share how you did it. I am going to watch you and if you need help, look at our anchor charts, ask a math partner and of course you can ask me.

Figure 5.24 Student Activities

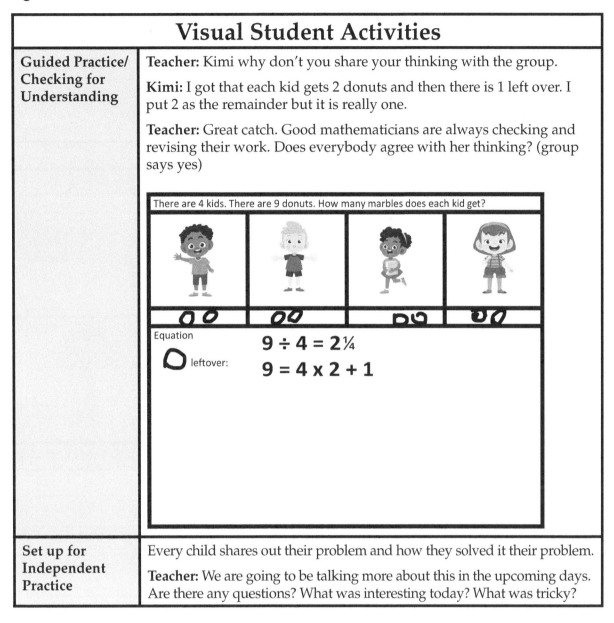

Guided Practice/ Checking for Understanding	**Teacher:** Kimi why don't you share your thinking with the group. **Kimi:** I got that each kid gets 2 donuts and then there is 1 left over. I put 2 as the remainder but it is really one. **Teacher:** Great catch. Good mathematicians are always checking and revising their work. Does everybody agree with her thinking? (group says yes)
Set up for Independent Practice	Every child shares out their problem and how they solved it their problem. **Teacher:** We are going to be talking more about this in the upcoming days. Are there any questions? What was interesting today? What was tricky?

Figure 5.25 Lesson Close

Close

♦ What did we do today?
♦ What was the math we were practicing?
♦ What were we doing with our number wands?
♦ Was this easy or tricky?
♦ Turn to a partner and state one thing you learned today.

Figure 5.26 More Examples of Division Mats

leftover

Equation:

There is a remainder of _____

leftover

Equation:

There is a remainder of _____

Abstract Lesson

Figure 5.27 Abstract Introduction

Introduction to Abstract Explorations

Launch	**Teacher:** Today we are going to continue to work on division. **Vocabulary:** dividend, divisor, quotient, expression, equation **Math Talk:** The quotient is _____. The dividend is ____. The divisor is ____.
Model	**Teacher:** There are many different things that you can do when you have a remainder. Today we are going to tell stories where we think and talk about that. Tell me a story where you have to keep the remainder. Let's talk about pencils. **Tommy:** There were 10 pencils. Mrs. Chi is going to put 3 in a box. How many boxes will she need? **Teddy:** She will need 4 boxes… see 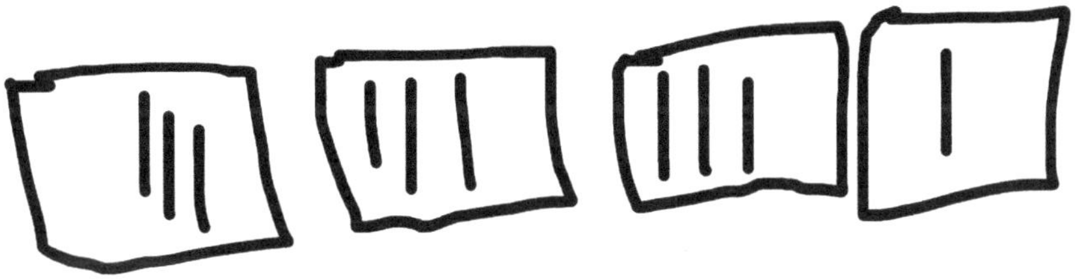
Checking for Understanding	**Teacher:** Yes! We can't throw that pencil away so we need a 4th box for it.

Figure 5.28 Student Activity

Visual Student Activity	
Guided Practice/ Checking for Understanding	**Teacher:** There were 10 pencils. There were 4 kids. How many can each kid get if they all get the same amount. The teacher will keep the extras.
	Tiffany: Each kid will get 2 and the teacher will keep 2. See…
Set up for Independent Practice	**Teacher:** So, when we have a remainder there are lots of different things that can happen to it depending on what the problem is asking. Who can tell me more about that?
	Tami: Sometimes you drop it.
	Mike: Sometimes you have to include it.
	Teddy: Sometimes you can share it…like the problem we did on the rug.
	After all the students share, the teacher wraps up the lesson and the students go to their workstations.

Figure 5.29 Lesson Close

Close
♦ What did we do today? ♦ What was the math we were practicing? ♦ What were we doing with our number wands? ♦ Was this easy or tricky? ♦ Turn to a partner and state one thing you learned today.

Section Summary

Division is tricky for students. They must have plenty of opportunities where they get to act out word problems. The problems should be real-life contexts so that students can understand what they are talking about. They should act out the problem with manipulatives, then sketch out the problems and finally be able to solve the problems with symbols. Students should be able to talk about the relationships between concrete, pictorial and abstract representations of the same problem.

Subtraction Across Zeros

Overview

Figure 5.30 Overview

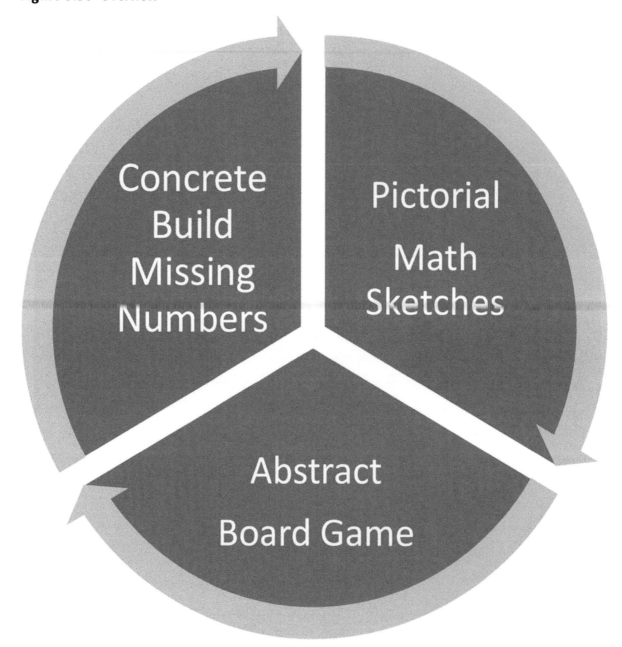

Figure 5.31 Planning Template

Subtraction Across Zeros

Big Idea: Numbers, Operation Meanings & Relationships; Properties, Basic Facts & Algorithms **Enduring Understanding:** Students will understand that they can solve problems with zeros in the minuend. **Essential Question:** How do we use subtraction in our everyday lives? **I can statement:** I can use different strategies to subtract across zeros.	**Materials** Tools: counters (tiles, cubes, circles) --- **Vocabulary & Language Frames** **Vocabulary:** zeros, compensation, regrouping, math sketch, count up, count back, strategy, model **Math Talk:** My strategy was _____. My model was _____.

Cycle of Engagement

		Abstract:	Math Processes/ Practices
$1000 - 590$ Count up 10 gets you to 600 plus 400 more makes 1000 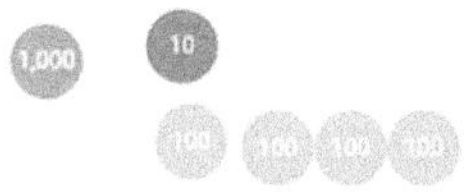	Pictorial $205 - 162$ Count up Difference is 38 	$200 - 156 = 199 - 155$	♦ **Problem Solving** ♦ **Reasoning** ♦ **Models** ♦ **Tools** ♦ **Precision** ♦ **Structure** ♦ **Pattern**

Figure 5.32 Differentiation

3 Differentiated Lessons		
In this series of lessons, students are working on subtracting across zeros. Students should be developing this concept through concrete activities, pictorial activities and abstract activities. Here are some things to think about as you do these lessons.		
Emerging	**On Grade Level**	**Above Grade Level**
Do a lot of work with manipulatives.	Do a lot of work with different manipulatives and having the students do math sketches.	Talk about different models. Work with larger numbers.

 Looking for Misunderstandings and Common Errors

Students have trouble with understanding regrouping with more than one zero. Start with numbers that are small enough to be broken up with place value blocks before moving onto sketching problem with the same amounts.

Figure 5.33 Anchor Chart

Concrete	Abstract
2000 – 1,150 Just count up from 1,150 to 2000 You will get 850 	

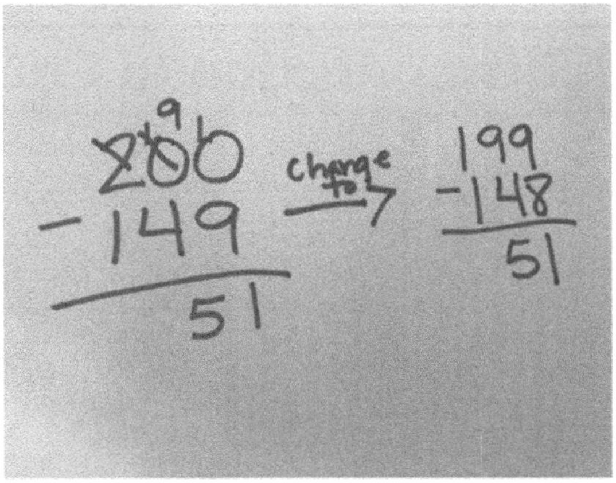

Pictorial	
201 - 99 201 – 100 = 101 101 + 1 = 102 I took too many away so I add 1 back	

Concrete Lesson

Figure 5.34 Concrete Introduction

Introduction to Concrete Explorations

Launch	**Teacher:** Today we are going to work on subtracting across zeros. A lot of students have trouble with this so we are going to look at a strategy that might help you. **Vocabulary:** subtrahend, minuend, minus, take away, subtract, zero, regroup, **Math Talk:** I made an easier problem. I regrouped the numbers.
Model	**Teacher:** Today we are going to explore subtracting across zeros with base ten blocks. Let's look at this problem. We have 200 but we need to break one of the hundreds into tens. So we still have the same amount but instead of 2 hundreds we have 1 hundred and 10 tens.  **Teacher:** Now we have to break one of those tens into 10 ones. And now we can take away 33. How much do we have left? **Tyler:** We have 167 left. We can check it by adding 33 plus 167 and that makes 200. 
Checking for Understanding	*Teacher reads 2 more problems that the group discusses.* **Teacher:** Ok. I am going to give each one of you your own problem. I want you to solve it. Be ready to share how you did it. I am going to watch you and if you need help, look at our anchor charts, ask a math partner and of course you can ask me.

Figure 5.35 Student Activity

	Concrete Student Activities
Guided Practice/ Checking for Understanding	**Teacher:** Let's look at another problem. Terri explain what we all did. **Terri:** First we had 200. Then we broke one of the hundreds into 10 tens. And then we took away 57. We have 143 left. 
Set up for Independent Practice	Every child shares out their problem and how they solved it. We are going to be talking more about that in the upcoming days. Are there any questions? What was interesting today? What was tricky?

Figure 5.36 Lesson Close

Close
◆ What did we do today? ◆ What was the math we were practicing? ◆ What were we doing with our place value blocks? ◆ Was this easy or tricky? ◆ Turn to a partner and state one thing you learned today.

Figure 5.37 Place Value Mat

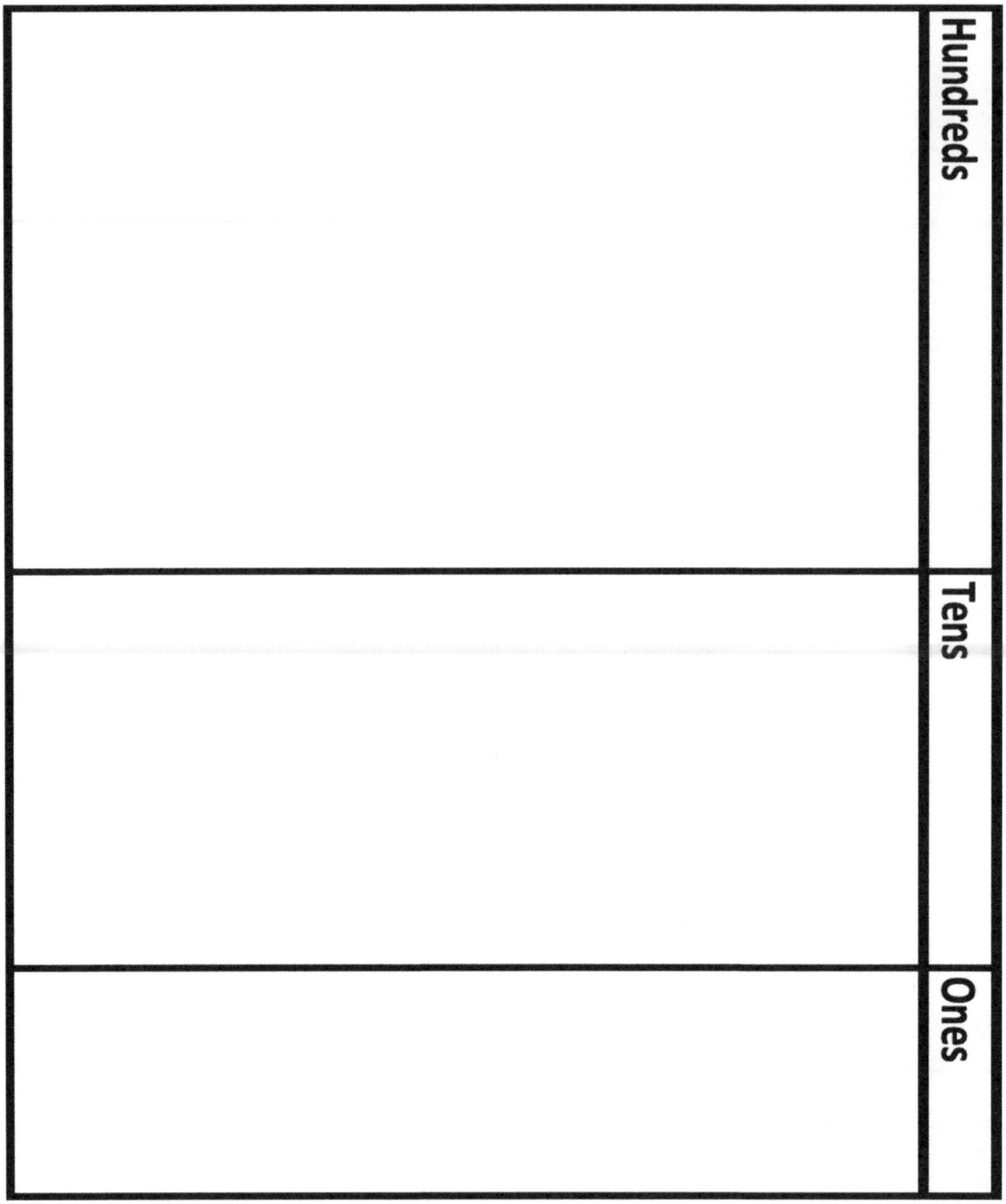

Visual Lesson

Figure 5.38 Visual Introduction

Introduction to a Visual Explorations

Launch	**Teacher:** Today we are going to work on subtracting across zeros. **Vocabulary**: subtrahend, minuend, minus, take away, subtract, zero, regroup, **Math Talk:** I made an easier problem. I regrouped the numbers.
Model	**Teacher:** Today we are going to look at sketching out the problem. Our first problem is 300 – 154. Let's sketch it out. First we are going to draw the 300. Now how are we going to take away 154. Who can explain what happened in this drawing? **Teddy:** We are going to have to break apart 2 of the hundreds into tens. **Claire:** And then we have to break a ten into ten ones. **Maria:** And then we can take away 154 and we have 46 left. 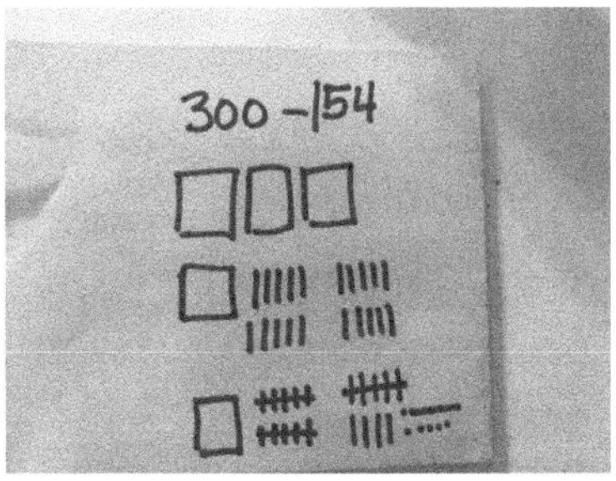
Checking for Understanding	**Teacher:** Ok. I am going to give each one of you your own problem. I want you to solve it. Model it with a sketch and then be ready to share how you did it. I am going to watch you and if you need help, look at our anchor charts, ask a math partner and of course you can ask me.

Figure 5.39 Student Activity

	Visual Student Activity
Guided Practice/ Checking for Understanding	**Teacher:** Kay explain your problem to us. **Kay:** I had 100 take away 78. First I drew 100 but I had to break it up into tens. And then I had to break 1 ten into 10 ones. I got 22 left. 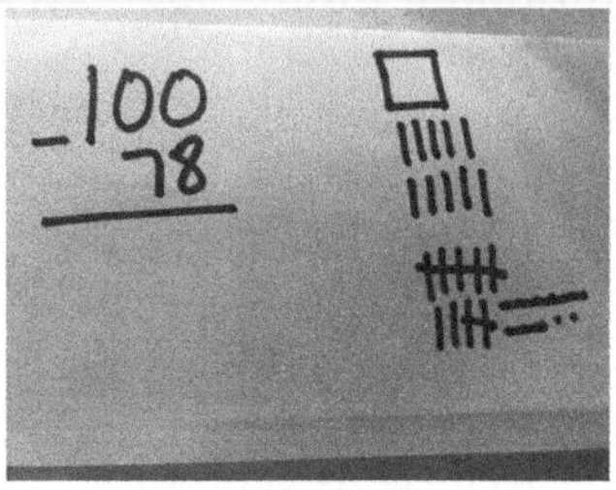
Set up for Independent Practice	*Teacher gives everybody a chance to do and discuss a problem. After everyone has shared the lesson ends.* ***Teacher:*** *We are going to be talking more about this in the upcoming days. Are there any questions? What was interesting today? What was tricky?*

Figure 5.40 Lesson Close

Close
♦ What did we do today? ♦ What was the math we were practicing? ♦ What were we doing with our sketches? ♦ Was this easy or tricky? ♦ Turn to a partner and state one thing you learned today.

Figure 5.41 Problem Solving Mat

Equation	
Drawing 1	
Drawing 2	
Drawing 3	

Abstract Lesson

Figure 5.42 Abstract Introduction

<table>
<tr><td colspan="2"><h2 align="center">Introduction to Abstract Explorations</h2></td></tr>
<tr>
<td>Launch</td>
<td>

Teacher: Today we are going to work on subtracting across zeros. A lot of students have trouble with this so we are going to look at a strategy that might help you.

Vocabulary: subtrahend, minuend, minus, take away, subtract, zero, regroup,

Math Talk:
I made an easier problem.
I regrouped the numbers.

</td>
</tr>
<tr>
<td>Model</td>
<td>

Teacher: Let's look at this problem:
50 – 17…. How might we solve it?

Kayla: We could count up…. Like plus 3 is 20 and then 30 more so the difference is 33.

Teddy: We could just subtract (he does traditional algorithm)

Teacher: We could also make it an easier problem. We could add 3 to 17 to make it 20 and remember when we are subtracting what we do to one number we have to do to the other… so we can change the problem into an equivalent problem… 53 – 20 which is way easier….Does everybody see that? Let's try another one….
90 – 53….

Tim: We could add 7 to make the 53 a 60 and then add 7 to 90 so we get 97 – 60…that's easy… that's 37….

Teacher: Let's do a bigger problem… 700 – 552…

Jamal: Well, I would count up… 48 to 600 plus 100 more to 700… so the difference is 148

Harry: Or, we could add 48 to each one and make it 748 – 600…

</td>
</tr>
<tr>
<td>Checking for Understanding</td>
<td>

Teacher: Let's look at this problem:
50 – 17…. We could also subtract 1 from this problem…watch… we could make the problem

</td>
</tr>
</table>

Figure 5.42 (Continued)

	49 – 16 and the answer is 33…. Let's do another one…. 500 – 482…. Let's try it by taking away 1 from each….
	Teddy: So 499 – 481…that's 18…
	Mark: You could also count up from 482… to 490 and then 500 and that would also be 18
	Teacher: Yes, so there are all these ways we can think about subtracting across zeros without getting bogged down in all that regrouping…. Let's try another one….. 8000 – 4578…
	Grace: 7999 – 4577… that's easier… 3,422…..

Figure 5.43 Student Activity

	<div align="center">**Abstract Student Activity**</div>
Guided Practice/ Checking for Understanding	**Teacher:** Today we are going to play a board game with a focus on subtracting across zeros. You roll and then move. When you land you have to solve the problem and explain your thinking to your math partner. I want you to think about some of the strategies we have been talking about today. Whoever gets to Finish first wins. The focus is to explain your strategy for solving the problem. Your partner can check your work with the calculator. If you are correct you stay where you moved, if you are incorrect you move back 1 space. 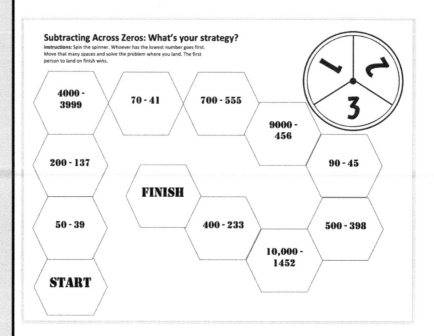 **Teacher:** Misha tell me how you solved that problem. **Misha:** I had 700 take away 555. I know that 45 more is 600 and then 100 more to 700 so the difference is 145.
Set up for Independent Practice	The teacher continues to ask the students questions about their strategies as they play the game. The teacher is taking notes as the students play. They are using their different strategies to explain their thinking.

Figure 5.44 Lesson Close

Close
♦ What did we do today?
♦ What was the math we were practicing?
♦ How did we model the math?
♦ Was this easy or tricky?
♦ Turn to a partner and state one thing you learned today.

Figure 5.45 Gameboard

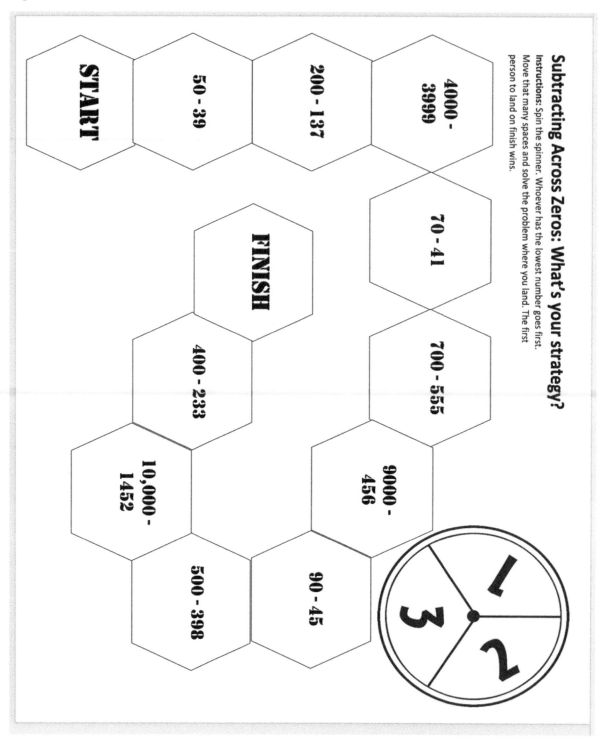

Subtracting Across Zeros: What's your strategy?

Instructions: Spin the spinner. Whoever has the lowest number goes first. Move that many spaces and solve the problem where you land. The first person to land on finish wins.

START

50 - 39

200 - 137

4000 - 3999

70 - 41

700 - 555

FINISH

400 - 233

9000 - 456

10,000 - 1452

90 - 45

500 - 398

Section Summary

Subtracting across zeros is a very tricky concept for students. Many of them get tripped up trying to do regrouping all the way across from second grade through fifth. So, it is important that students have different strategies for approaching these problems. They should review working with place value blocks because it reinforces what they are doing when they are just working with numbers. Place value blocks and math sketches help students to see the regrouping in action. Having strategies such as compensation or counting up when working with just the numbers is also very important. Review this skill and these strategies throughout the year.

Division of a Double-Digit Number by a Single-Digit Number

Overview

Figure 5.46 Overview

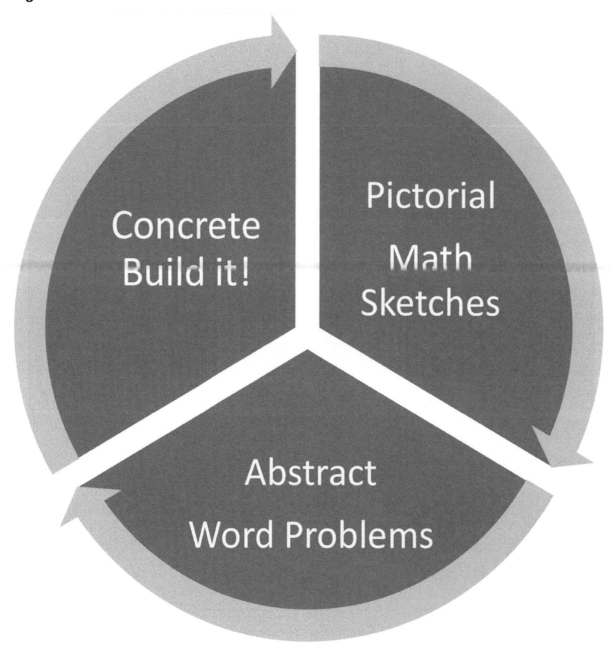

Figure 5.47 Planning Template

Division of Two-digit Numbers

Big Idea: Numbers, Operation Meanings & Relationships; Properties, Basic Facts & Algorithms **Enduring Understanding:** Students will understand different ways to model and represent division of multi-digit numbers. **Essential Question:** Why is division important? How do we use it in real life? **I can statement:** I can show different ways to model division of a 2-digit number by a 1-digit number.	**Materials** ♦ Tools: counters (tiles, cubes, circles) **Vocabulary & Language Frames** **Vocabulary:** divisor, dividend, quotient, partial quotients, model, strategy **Math Talk:** The quotient is _____. The remainder is _____.
Cycle of Engagement **Concrete:** 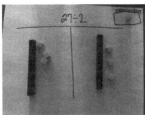 $27 \div 2$ **Pictorial:** 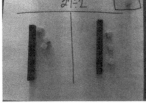 **Abstract:** $27 \div 2 = 13\frac{1}{2}$ or $27 = 2 \times 13 + 1$	**Math Processes/Practices** ♦ **Problem Solving** ♦ **Reasoning** ♦ **Models** ♦ **Tools** ♦ **Precision** ♦ **Structure** ♦ **Pattern**

Figure 5.48 Differentiation

| 3 Differentiated Lessons |
| In this series of lessons, students are working on dividing double-digit numbers by single-digit numbers. They are developing this concept through concrete activities, pictorial activities and abstract activities. Here are some things to think about as you do these lessons. |

Emerging	On Grade Level	Above Grade Level
Do a lot of work with manipulatives. Review basic division within 100.	Do a lot of work with different manipulatives and having the students do math sketches. Make sure to scaffold the concept by first focusing intensely on 2-digit numbers and then only moving to 3 and 4 digit numbers when students thoroughly understand and can explain what they are doing.	Talk about different models. Work with larger numbers.

 # Looking for Misunderstandings and Common Errors

Students have trouble with division in general. Start with small numbers and problems that they can visualize before going on to larger numbers. Although most of the time, we see the remainder written like 3r1 it is not mathematically correct. It should be written like this: $14 = 4 \times 3 + 2$. I have also seen it written as $3 + r2$...or you can write it as a fraction or decimal.

Figure 5.49 Anchor Chart

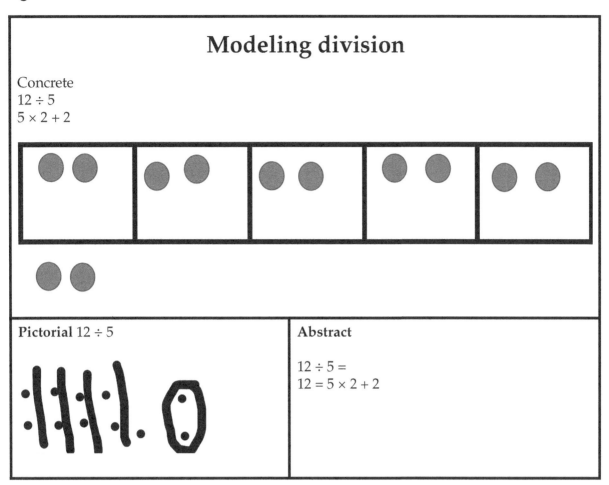

Modeling division

Concrete
12 ÷ 5
5 × 2 + 2

Pictorial 12 ÷ 5	Abstract
	12 ÷ 5 = 12 = 5 × 2 + 2

Concrete Lessons

Figure 5.50 Concrete Introduction

Introduction to a Concrete Exploration

Launch	**Teacher:** Today we are going to work on remainder stories. **Vocabulary:** dividend, divisor, quotient, expression, equation **Math Talk:** The quotient is _____. The dividend is _____. The divisor is _____.
Model	**Teacher:** Let's all take our mats. Count out 42 and divide it on the Division by 4 mat. What do you notice? **Ivan:** I see that it is 10 with a remainder of 2. 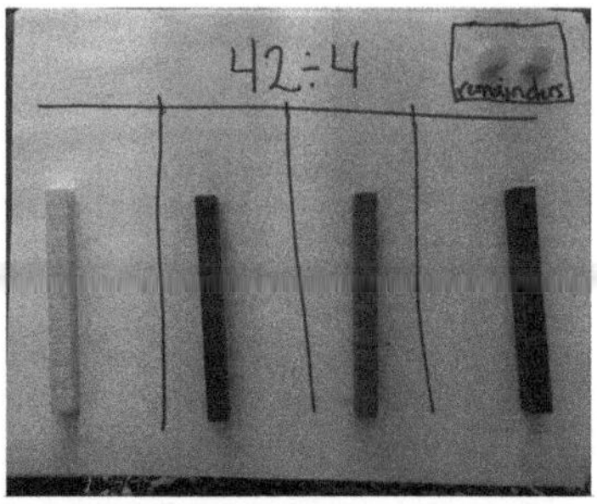
Checking for Understanding	**Teacher:** Ok, here is another problem. Who wants to explain what they did? **Johnny:** I do. I got 13 with a remainder of 1. 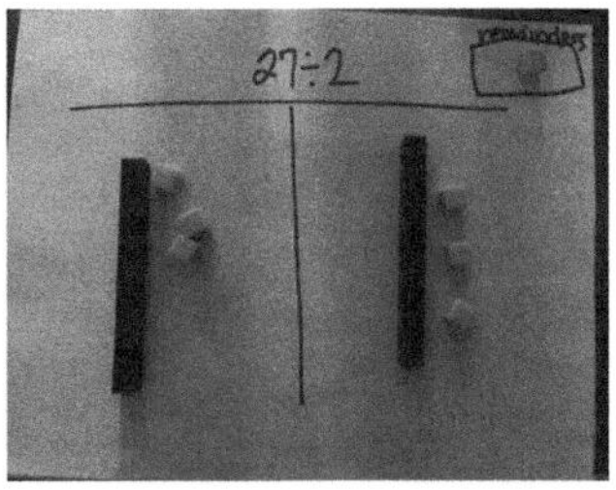 **Teacher:** Ok. I am going to give each one of you your own problem. I want you to read it. Solve it. Be ready to share how you did it. I am going to watch you and if you need help, look at our anchor charts and of course you can ask me.

Figure 5.51 Student Activity

	Concrete Student Activity
Guided Practice/ Checking for Understanding	Students act out various problems and the teacher watches, takes notes and asks the students questions. **Teacher:** Marcos, tell me how you solved that. **Marcos:** I had 34 divided by 3. I got 11 in each group with a remainder of 1. I know that 3 × 11 is 33 and then 1 more is 34 so my answer makes sense. 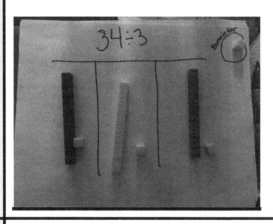
Set up for Independent Practice	*Teacher gives everybody a chance to do and discuss a problem. After everyone has shared the lesson ends.* *Teacher: We are going to be talking more about this in the upcoming days. Are there any questions? What was interesting today? What was tricky?*

Figure 5.52 Lesson Close

Close
♦ What did we do today? ♦ What was the math we were practicing? ♦ What were we doing with our place value blocks? ♦ Was this easy or tricky? ♦ Turn to a partner and state one thing you learned today.

Figure 5.53 Sample Division Cards

Problem:		
Solution:		

Visual Lessons

Figure 5.54 Visual Introduction

Introduction to Visual Explorations

Launch	**Teacher:** Today we are going to work on remainder stories. **Vocabulary:** dividend, divisor, quotient, expression, equation **Math Talk:** The quotient is _____. The dividend is _____. The divisor is _____.
Model	**Teacher:** Today we are going to model division with math sketches. I want you to solve this problem and then somebody share their thinking. **Maite:** I got 11 with a remainder of 3. I can check it with multiplication. 3 × 11 is 33 and then 3 more is 36…wait…so my remainder should be 2. **Dan:** Good catch! 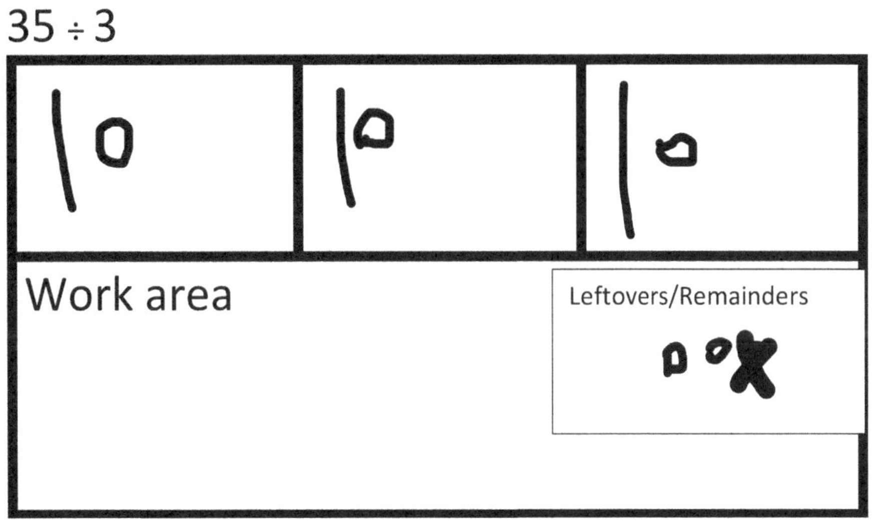 $35 \div 3$
Checking for Understanding	Students do 2 more problems together and then the teacher lets them work on their own.

Figure 5.55 Student Activity

	Pictorial Student Activity
Guided Practice/ Checking for Understanding	**Teacher:** Hong, tell me how you solved that problem. **Hong:** I got 16 with a remainder of 3. I can check it with multiplication so 4 × 14 is 64 and then 3 more would make it 67. # 67 ÷ 4 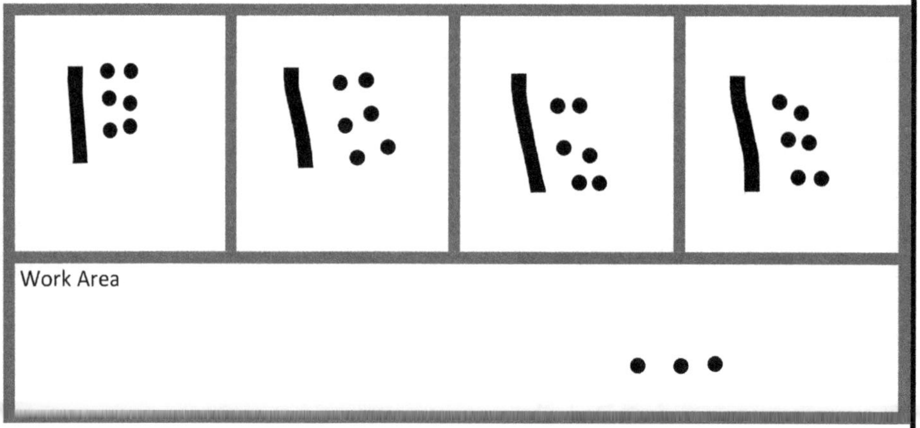 Work Area
Set up for Independent Practice	*Teacher gives everybody a chance to do and discuss a problem. After everyone has shared the lesson ends.* We are going to be talking more about this in the upcoming days. Are there any questions? What was interesting today? What was tricky?

Figure 5.56 Lesson Close

Close
◆ What did we do today? ◆ What was the math we were practicing? ◆ What were we doing with our place value blocks? ◆ Was this easy or tricky? ◆ Turn to a partner and state one thing you learned today.

Figure 5.57 Example of Division Mat

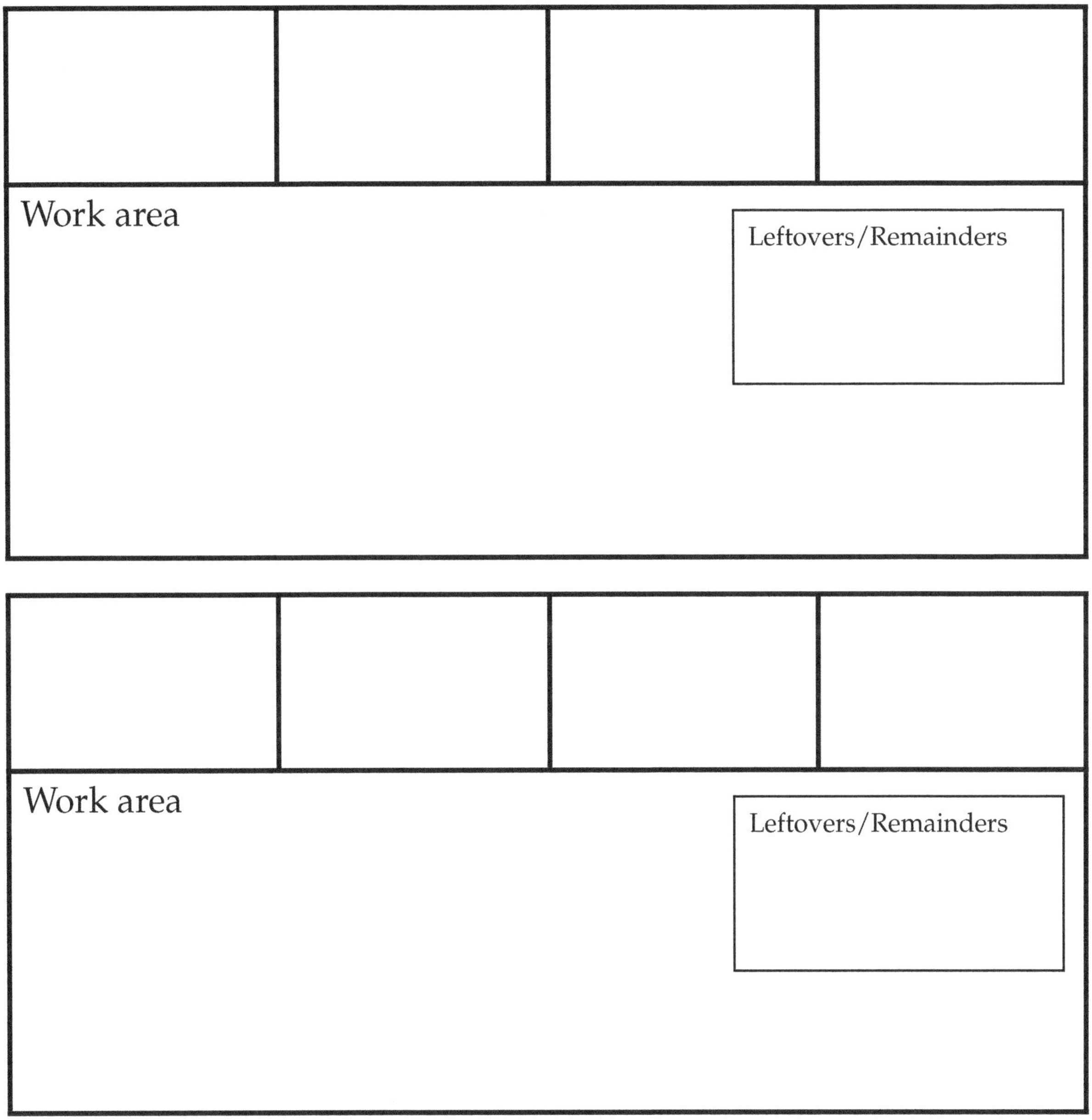

Work area			Leftovers/Remainders

Work area			Leftovers/Remainders

Abstract Lessons

Figure 5.58 Abstract Introduction

Introduction to Abstract Explorations

Launch	**Teacher:** Today we are going to work on remainder stories. **Vocabulary:** dividend, divisor, quotient, expression, equation **Math Talk:** The quotient is _____. The dividend is _____. The divisor is _____.
Model	**Teacher:** Today we are going to model division with open arrays. These are a way to show division with rectangles. So for example, let's look at a problem we looked at yesterday: $67 \div 4$. The question is how can we break this problem up into easier problems? Think tens. Can we take 40 out of 67? **Tami:** Yes. **Teacher:** So let's draw that: 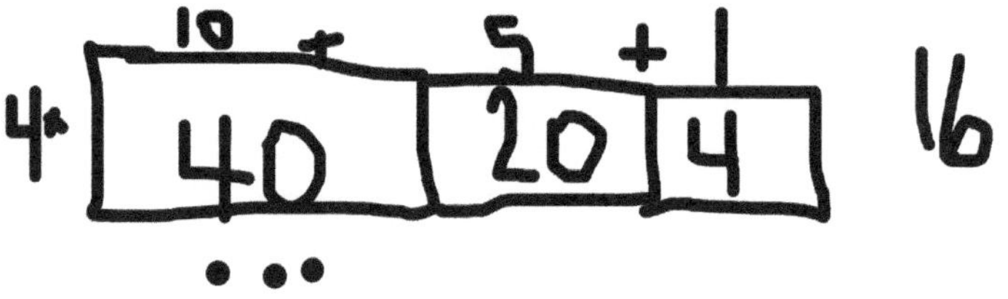
Checking for Understanding	**Teacher:** Can we take another 40? (students say no) right, how much is left? **Katie:** 27 **Teacher:** What can we take out of 27 that is easy to divide by 4. Use your multiplication tables to think about it? **Tim:** 20 **Teacher:** Ok, let's try that…. As you do add to the open array…. Now what do we have left…7…. So what can we take out of 7….

Figure 5.58 (Continued)

	Yesenia: 4 and 3 are left….
	Teacher: Notice our drawing we broke it into 40 and 20 and 4…. And we know that 4×10 is 40 and 4×5 is 20 and 4×1 is 4… so we have partial quotients….now we have to add them all together to get our total quotient…. And see if there are any leftovers….
	Mike: There are 3 leftovers…there is a remainder of 3
	Teacher: So today we are looking at how you can break apart a dividend to make it easier to divide. You can then divide it in parts and then put those parts back together.

Figure 5.59 Student Activity

Abstract Student Activity

Guided Practice/ Checking for Understanding	**Teacher:** Ok, let's do another problem: $38 \div 5$. **John:** I'll explain. Well 5×7 is 35 so you can take out 35 and then you have 3 left. $38 \div 5 = \underline{}$ 7 35 3
Set up for Independent Practice	The teacher continues to ask the students questions about their strategies as they work on problems. After they finish, the students go to various workstations.

Figure 5.60 Lesson Close

Close

- What did we do today?
- What was the math we were practicing?
- What were we doing with our sketches? Open array?
- Was this easy or tricky?
- Turn to a partner and state one thing you learned today.

Section Summary

Open arrays are part of the math standards in fourth grade, but many people do not teach them. As teachers, we all must get more comfortable doing them and coming up with strategies for breaking apart numbers. This can be tricky for teachers because most of us did not learn this way. So, we have to learn it so we can teach it to our students. It is really important to spend time working on breaking apart numbers in different ways. The idea of partial quotients is a powerful concept, and we need to spend a great deal more time than we usually do on it in schools. There are more and more great videos now on teaching with open arrays as well.

Depth of Knowledge

Depth of Knowledge is a framework that encourages us to ask questions that require students think, reason, explain, defend and justify their thinking (Webb, 2002). Here is snapshot of what that can look like in terms of place value work (see Figures 5.61 and 5.62).

Figure 5.61 DOK Activities

	What are different strategies and models that we can use to teach multiplicative comparison?	What are different strategies and models that we can use to teach division with remainders?	What are different strategies and models to teach subtraction across zeros?	What are different strategies and models to teach division of a double-digit number by a single-digit number?
Dok Level 1 (these are questions where students are required to simply recall/ reproduce an answer/do a procedure)	Solve: Sue had 2 marbles. Her sister had 2 times as many as she did. How many did she have?	Solve: 38 ÷ 5.	Solve: 300 - 129	Solve: 77÷ 9
Dok Level 2 (these are questions where students have to use information, think about concepts and reason) This is considered a more challenging problem than a level 1 problem.	Solve: Sue had 2 marbles. Her sister had 2 times as many as she did. How many did they have altogether? Model and explain your thinking.	Solve: 38 ÷ 5 and model and explain your thinking.	Solve: 300 – 129 in 2 different ways. Model and explain your thinking.	Solve: 77÷ 9 in 2 different ways. Model and explain your thinking.
Dok Level 3 (these are questions where students have to reason, plan, explain, justify and defend their thinking)	Write and solve a word problem where someone has 3 times as much as the other person.	Write and solve a word problem where the quotient is 4 with a remainder of 2.	Write and solve a word problem with zeros in the minuend and 9's in the subtrahend.	Write and solve a word problem where you divide a 2 or 3 digit number by a 1 digit number.

Source: A great resource for asking open questions is Marion Small's *Good Questions: Great ways to differentiate mathematics instruction in the standards-based classroom* (2017). Also, Robert Kaplinsky has done a great job in pushing our thinking forward with the Depth of Knowledge Matrices he created. The Kentucky Department of Education (2007) has a great document illustrating DOK Matrices.

Figure 5.62 Asking Rigorous Questions

Dok 1	Dok 2 At this level students explain their thinking.	Dok 3 At this level students have to justify, defend and prove their thinking with objects, drawings and diagrams.
What is the answer to ??? Can you model the number? Can you model the problem? Can you identify the answer that matches this equation? How many hundreds, tens and ones are in this number?	How do you know that the equation is correct? Can you pick the correct answer and explain why it is correct? How can you model that problem? What is another way to model that problem? Can you model that on the ....??? Give me an example of a ...type of problem.... Which answer is incorrect? Explain your thinking?	Can you prove that your answer is correct? Prove that... Explain why that is the answer... Show me how to solve that and explain what you are doing.

Key Points

♦ Building arrays
♦ Division
♦ Missing numbers
♦ Distributive property

Chapter Summary

Fluency is very important in third grade. It is much more than just knowing what the answer is to a problem. Students have to be able to contextualize problems. They should be able to tell stories about addition, subtraction, multiplication and division. They should have plenty of opportunities to work on missing numbers and make the connections between the operations. They should understand the properties. They should work with concrete manipulatives, do math sketches and work with symbols. This takes time across the year.

Reflection Questions

1. How are you currently doing fluency lessons?
2. Are you making sure that you do concrete, pictorial and abstract activities?
3. What do your students struggle with the most, and what ideas are you taking away from this chapter that might inform your work around those struggles?

References

Baroody, A. J., Purpura, D. J., Eiland, M. D., Reid, E. E., & Paliwal, V. (2016). Does fostering reasoning strategies for relatively difficult basic combinations promote transfer? *Journal of Educational Psychology, 108*(4), 576–591. doi:10.17105/SPR44-1.41-59

Bay-Williams, J., & Kling, B. (2019). *Math fact fluency*. Reston, VA: ASCD.

Boaler, J. (2015). *Fluency without fear: Research evidence on the best ways to learn math facts*. Retrieved September 6, 2019 from www.youcubed.org/evidence/fluency-without-fear/

Brownell, W. A. (1956, October). Meaning and skill—maintaining the balance. *Arithmetic Teacher, 3*, 129–136.

Brownell, W. A., & Chazal, C. B. (1935, September). The effects of premature drill in third-grade arithmetic. *Journal of Educational Research, 29*, 17–28.

Godfrey, C., & Stone, J. (2013). Mastering fact fluency: Are they game? *Teaching Children Mathematics, 20*(2), 96–101.

Henry, V., & Brown, R. (2008). First-grade basic facts: An investigation into teaching and learning of an accelerated, high-demand memorization standard. *Journal for Research in Mathematics Education, 30*(2), 1153–1183.

Kentucky Department of Education. (2007). *Support materials for core content for assessment version 4.1 mathematics*. Retrieved January 15, 2017.

Mathematics Learning Study Committee, Center for Education, Division of Behavioral and Social Sciences and Education, National Research Council, Kilpatrick, J., Swafford, J., & Findell, B. (Eds.). (2001). *Adding it up: helping children learn mathematics*. Washington, DC: National Academy Press.

National Center for Education Evaluation and Regional Assistance. (2009). *Assisting students struggling with mathematics: Response to Intervention (RtI) for elementary and middle schools. 2009–4060*. Retrieved IES from http://ies.ed.gov/ncee and http://ies.ed.gov/ncee/wwc/publications/practiceguides/

National Council of Teachers of Mathematics. (2000). *Principles and standards for school mathematics*. Reston, VA: National Council of Teachers of Mathematics.

Newton, R. (2016). *Math running records*. New York: Routledge.

Newton, R., Record, A., & Mello, A. (2020). *Fluency doesn't just happen*. New York: Routledge.

Thornton, C. (1978). Emphasizing thinking strategies in basic fact instruction. *Journal for Research in Mathematics Education*, 9(3), 214–225. Reston, VA: NCTM.

Van de Walle, J. A. (2007). *Elementary and middle school mathematics: Teaching developmentally*. Boston, MA: Pearson / Allyn and Bacon.

Webb, N. (2002). *An analysis of the alignment between mathematics standards and assessments for three states*. Paper presented at the annual meeting of the American Educational Research Association, New Orleans, LA.

6

Small Group Word Problem Lessons

It is important to teach about word problems in small guided math groups. Word problems have a specific learning trajectory as outlined in the *Cognitively Guided Instruction* work (Carpenter, Fennema, Franke, Levi, & Empson, 1999/2015). There are specific categories and levels of problems. Students should get an opportunity to explore solving various problems in various ways. This work should be scaffolded in the guided math group.

Every state has outlined the types of problems by grades that students should be working on. In the guided math group, teachers scaffold the learning so that students are working in their zone of proximal development towards the grade level standards. The reality is that some problems are more challenging than others. Also, even within categories, number ranges can vary and should be scaffolded.

We also look at a few traditional problems about time and measurement. We do 3 read protocol problems where students have to make the questions and then solve them. We also look at open problems, where there is context and then students make up the entire problem and solve it on a model. We also look at picture word problem prompts where students have to make up the story.

DOI: 10.4324/9781003169581-6

Research Note 🔍

♦ Students have a tendency to "suspend sense-making" when they are solving problems. They don't stop to reason through the problem (; Schoenfeld, 1992; Verschaffel, Greer, & De Corte, 2000). We must find ways to slow the process down so they can think.
♦ Students develop a "compulsion to calculate" (Stacey & MacGregor, 1999) that can interfere with the development of the algebraic thinking that is needed to solve word problems (cited in www.cde.state.co.us/comath/word-problems-guide).
♦ Research consistently states that we should **never use key words**. From the beginning, teach students to reason about the context, not to depend on key words. See a great blog post that cites many articles on this: https://gfletchy.com/2015/01/12/teaching-key-words-forget-about-it/

In this chapter we explore:

♦ Measurement problems
♦ Modeling multiplication word problems
♦ Elapsed time word problems whole
♦ 3 read problems
♦ Picture prompts (see Figures 6.1 to 6.55)

Measurement Problems

Overview

Figure 6.1 Overview

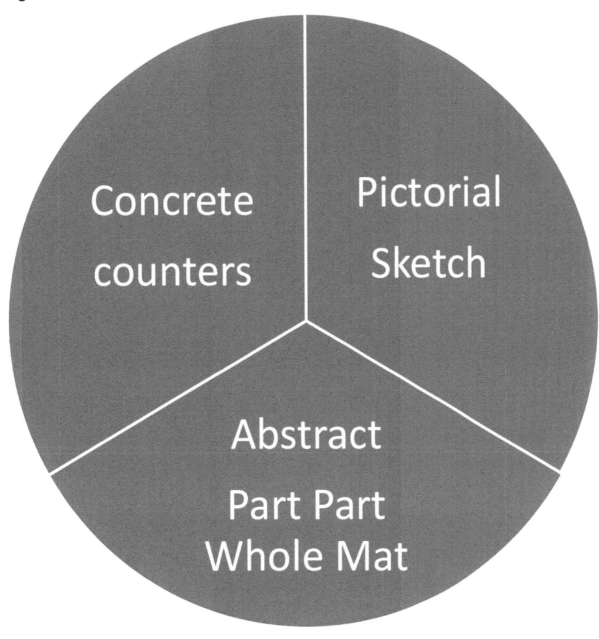

Figure 6.2 Planning Template

Measurement Start Unknown Word Problems

Big Idea: Numbers, Operation Meanings & Relationships **Enduring Understanding:** Students understand that there are many different ways to model problems. **Essential Question:** What are the ways to model measurement problems? **I can statement:** I can model measurement problems. I can use different strategies to solve measurement problems.	**Materials** ♦ Tools: Measurement Cups ♦ Templates: Measurement Cups ♦ Cards ♦ Crayons

Cycle of Engagement **Concrete:**  **Pictorial: Drawing**  **Abstract:** Sue poured some milk into the cake mix. Then, she poured 500 ml more. Now she has a 1.25 ml. How much did she start with?	Vocabulary & Language Frames ♦ Beakers ♦ Measurement Cups ♦ Start ♦ Change ♦ End ♦ Liters ♦ Milliliters **My strategy was _____.** **My model was _____.**

Figure 6.3 Three Differentiated Lessons

3 Differentiated Lessons
In this series of lessons, students are working on the concept of measurement problems. They are developing this concept through concrete activities, pictorial activities and abstract activities. Everybody should do the cycle. Some students progress through it more quickly than others. Here are some things to think about as you do these lessons.

Emergent	On Grade Level	Above Grade Level
Review adding. As you introduce this to students, do a lot of work by acting it out and then doing it with manipulatives. Be sure to have students draw what they acted out and connect it to number models.	The grade level standard is that students can model it and explain it. So do lots of this work where students are modeling it and explaining it.	Extend the number range.

 # Looking for Misunderstandings and Common Errors

Measurement is a very tricky topic for students. Students need to have hands on experiences with it. Students need concrete experiences with different types of measurement. They should act out the problems at the small group table amidst conversation and discussion about the topic.

Concrete Lesson

Figure 6.4 Introduction

	Introduction of Concrete Explorations: Open Measurement Problems
Launch	**Teacher:** Today we are going to do a measurement activity (make sure you send home letters about any allergies before you do this and get them signed by parents for participation). **Vocabulary:** milliliters, liters, capacity, measure **Math talk:** We used _____ ml. My model was … My strategy was….
Model	Today we are going to talk about making fruit punch. Grandma has 3 ingredients. She has some orange juice, some pineapple juice and some cranberry juice. She wants to make a liter of punch. What could some possibilities for the recipe be? Students taste test and work together to come up with a recipe for what the punch could be. They talk about what they like, what they don't like and what the strong flavor should be. They then try out the recipe at the table with the teacher asking questions.

Figure 6.4 (Continued)

	Record of Thinking	
	1st Try	2st Try

Checking for Understanding	**Teacher:** Who can tell me about one of your recipes?
	Maite: We tried 200 ml apple juice, 400 ml of orange juice and 400 ml of pineapple juice.
	Ted: We liked it!

Figure 6.5 Student Activity

	Concrete Student Activity
Guided Practice/ Checking for Understanding	The teacher passes out the problems. Students pull a card and act out their problems. The students each get a chance to share their problem and explain how they solved it. **Maria: My problem is this:** Luke drank 2.5 ml of water all day. How much could he have drank at different times? So, I looked at my measurement cup and I broke up 1000 ml. I said that he drank 700 ml of water in the morning and 800 ml of water at lunch and 1 liter in the evening. **Teacher:** What did you notice while looking at the measuring cup? **Maria:** I noticed how much a liter is. **Teacher:** What are some other things that you all noticed. **Hong:** I looked at the measuring cup and the bottle of water to tell my story. It is interesting to think about the amount.
Set up for Independent Practice	**Teacher:** That is great! We are going to continue working with the measuring cups in the workstations and also do some drawings.

Figure 6.6 Lesson Close

Close
♦ What did we do today? ♦ What was the math we were practicing? ♦ What were we doing with our measuring cups? ♦ Was this easy or tricky? ♦ Turn to a partner and state one thing you learned today.

Figure 6.7 Problem Cards

Mike drank a liter of water during the day. What are the different amounts that he could have drank throughout the day?	Carla drank 200 ml of water in the morning and then some more in the afternoon. Altogether she drank 1500 ml. How much did she drink in the afternoon?
Ricky drank 800 ml of water in the morning, and 300 ml of water in the afternoon. He drank some more in the evening. He drank a total of a liter and a half. How much did he drink in the afternoon?	Lucy drank 1100 ml of water. Mike drank a liter of water. Who drank more and how much more?
Mike drank 2 liters of water during the day. What are the different amounts that he could have drank throughout the day?	Carla drank some water in the morning and then 1.2 liters more in the afternoon. She drank a total of 2.5 liters of water. How much did she drink in the morning?
Ricky drank 900 ml of water in the morning, and 500 ml of water in the afternoon. He drank some more in the evening. He drank a total of 2 liters. How much did he drink in the evening?	Lucy drank ½ a liter of water. Mike drank 520 ml of water. Who drank more and how much more?

Visual (Pictorial) Lesson

Figure 6.8 Introduction

Introduction to Visual Explorations

Launch	**Teacher:** Today we are going to work on solving pictorial measurement activities. **Vocabulary: add, start, word problem, count up, number sentence (equation), missing number, gram (g), kilogram (kl),** **Math Talk: The weight is about ___ ounces.** **The weight is about _____ pounds.**
Model	**Teacher:** Today we are going to talk about mass. I am going to show you some things and then ask you what do you notice and what do you wonder about their mass.

<table>
<tr><th>Ounces</th><th>Pounds</th></tr>
<tr><td>Paper clip
Piece of paper
Penny Feather</td><td>A book
4 apples</td></tr>
</table>

Teacher: What do you notice about our things?

Ted: I noticed that ounces are light and pounds weigh more.

Teacher: Today you are going to take a walk around the room and then find and write down things that you would weigh in ounces and pounds. Here is your recording sheet. Sketch your object. When you come back be ready to defend your thinking.

Notes and Observations

Recording Sheet of things around the classroom

ounces	pounds

Checking for Understanding	*Students get up and walk around the room and write down different things either as being measured in ounces or pounds. Then they come back to talk about their observations and sketches.*

Figure 6.9 Student Activity

	Student Activity
Guided Practice/ Checking for Understanding	Everyone meets back at the table after about 5 minutes and they discuss their findings and their drawings. **Jamil:** I put a pencil as something we would weigh in ounces and the desk as something we would weight in pounds. The pencil is very light and the desk is very heavy compared to the pencil. **Recording Sheet of things around the classroom** <table><tr><td>ounces</td><td>pounds</td></tr><tr><td>Pencil Crayon Paper clip</td><td>Desk Chair door</td></tr><tr><td colspan="2">Notes and Observations Ounces are light and pounds are heavy.</td></tr></table> **Teacher:** Who agrees with him? **Grace:** I do. I put the crayon under ounces and the chair under pounds.
Set up for Independent Practice	*Teacher gives everybody a chance to discuss some of their observations and explain their thinking. After everyone has shared the lesson ends.* We are going to be talking more about this in the upcoming days. Are there any questions? What was interesting today? What was tricky?

Figure 6.10 Recording Sheet

Recording Sheet of things around the classroom	
Ounces	**Pounds**

Notes and Observations

Figure 6.11 Lesson Close

Close

- What did we do today?
- What was the math we were practicing?
- What were we doing with the objects around the room?
- Was this easy or tricky?
- Turn to a partner and state one thing you learned today.

Abstract Lesson

Figure 6.12 Abstract Introduction

	Introduction to Abstract Explorations	
Launch	**Teacher:** Today we are going to continue work on solving measurement word problems **Vocabulary: add, start unknown, word problem, count up, number sentence (equation)** **Math Talk:** **My strategy _____.** **I modeled my thinking by _____.** **I know my answer is correct because _____.**	
Model	**Teacher:** I am going to give you some word problems and we will reason them out with different models and tools. Here is one. *Mike made 2.5 liters punch. He then made a little more. Now he has 3.4 liters. How much more punch did he make?* **Ted:** Well, 500 ml would make 3 liters and then add 400 more liters. So that means he put in 900 ml.	
Checking for Understanding	**Teacher: Any other thoughts?** **Connie:** We could subtract 2.5 from 3.4 too. **Teacher:** Yes we could do that. I am going to read the problem and then you will model it in a part-part whole diagram and show it to the group. We will take turns explaining our thinking. Here we go.	

Figure 6.13 Student Activity

	Student Activity
Guided Practice/ Checking for Understanding	The teacher reads different problems. The children solve the problems however they want and then they solve them using different tools and models and show them and explain their thinking to the group. Each time, a different student explains how they solved the problem.

Josephine explains: I used a part-part whole mat. The problem said Grandma Mary made 1.5 liters of punch. Then she made some more. Now she has 3.9 liters of punch. How much more did she make? So, I can count up from 1.5 liters to 3.9. 500 more would be 2 liters. Then, 1000 more would be 3 liters. Then, 900 more would be 3.9 liters. So if I add it all up it is 2.4 liters that she put in.

3.9 liters	
1.5 liters	?

Teacher: Yes.

Everybody models the problems and show it on their part-part whole mat. Some students have the numbers in the wrong place and they erase and fix it. Teacher reminds everybody that it is ok to make mistakes because that means you are trying and when you keep trying you will get it.

Teacher: We are going to be talking more about this in the upcoming days. Are there any questions? What was interesting today? What was tricky?

Kelly: I think it is tricky to know where the numbers go.

Teacher: Yes it can be tricky. Who can give us some ideas on how to work with the numbers?

Jamal: You have to look at the total and that goes at the top. The other number is how many there were so that goes in this box. The missing number always goes wherever the part is that you are looking for. |
| **Set up for Independent Practice** | **Teacher:** Does it always go there or does it depend on what is happening in the problem?
Jamal: It depends on the what is happening in the problem.
Teacher: Ok then. Anymore comments or questions? If not, you all can go to your next station as soon as I ring the rotation bell. |

Figure 6.14 Lesson Close

Close
♦ What did we do today?
♦ What was the math we were practicing?
♦ What were we doing with our ml and L? part-part whole mat?
♦ Was this easy or tricky?
♦ Turn to a partner and state one thing you learned today.

Figure 6.15 Problem Solving Cards

500 ml + ___ L = 2.5 L	Luke made 500 ml of punch. He then put in some cranberry juice. Now he has 2.5 liters of punch. How much did he have in the beginning?
1.7 L + ? = 2.5 L	Luke made 1.7 liters of punch. He then added some cranberry juice. Now he has 2 ½ liters of punch. How much cranberry juice did he put in?
? + 1.6 = 2.20	Luke made punch. First he put in some orange juice. He then added 1.6 liters cranberry juice. Now he as 2.20 liters of punch. How much orange juice did he add?
500 + ? = 1.5	Luke made 500 ml of punch. He then put some cranberry juice. Now he has 1 ½ liters of punch. How much cranberry juice did he add?
? + 1.5 = 3.0	Jamal made some punch. First he added some mango juice. Then he added 1.5 liters of orange juice. Now he has 3.0 liters of punch. How much mango juice did he put in?

Section Summary

Measurement problems can be very tricky. Students have to not only work on what is happening in the situation of the problem, but they also are working with understanding metric units of measure and customary units of measure. Start Unknown problems can be very tricky. The Add to Start Unknown problems should be scaffolded with counters and in part-part whole mats. The counters provide that physical contact so students can move them around to make sense of the problem. The part-part whole mat is a great abstract visual because students can see the numbers. Number lines and number grids are also great abstract visual scaffolds because students can see the numbers. Eventually you want students to be able to reason it out with just equations and/or mental math.

Modeling Multiplication Word Problems

Overview

Figure 6.16 Overview

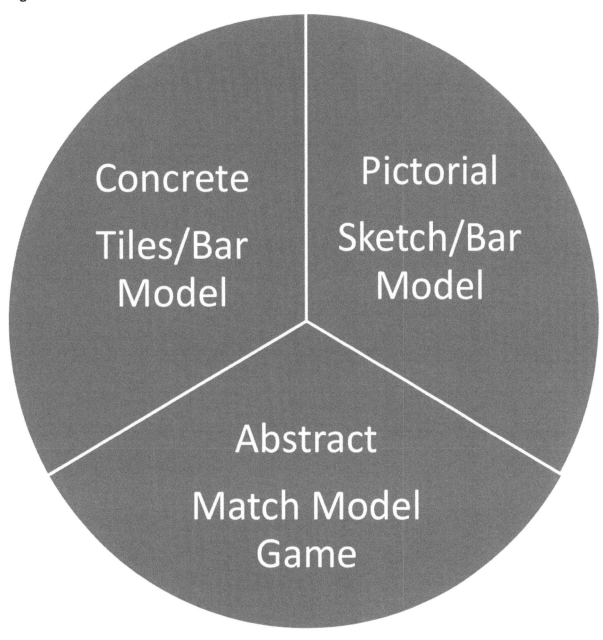

Figure 6.17 Planning Template

Multiplication Problems with Tape Diagram

Big Idea: Numbers; Operation Meanings & Relationships **Enduring Understanding:** We can model problems in many ways. **Essential Question:** What are the ways to model this type of problem? **I can statement:** I can model problems with tape/bar diagrams	**Materials** ♦ Tools: 1-inch tiles, 1-inch grid paper ♦ Cards ♦ Crayons

Cycle of Engagement

Concrete:

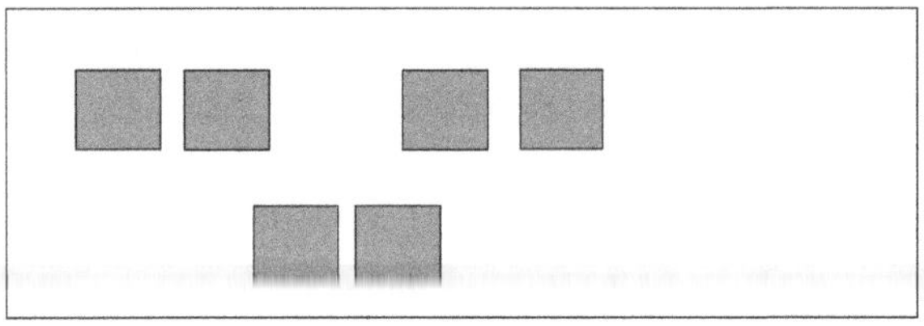

Pictorial: Drawing

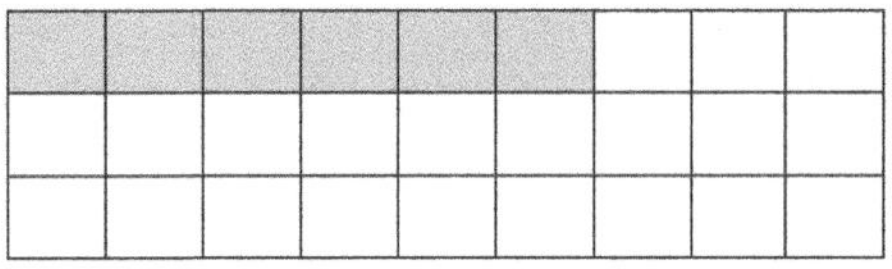

Vocabulary & Language Frames

♦ One-inch tile model
♦ Tape Diagram

My model is….
My strategy is ….

Abstract: Bar diagram

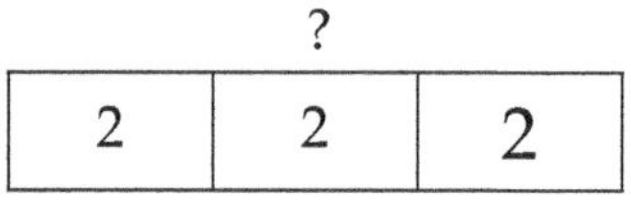

?

2	2	2

Figure 6.18 Differentiation

3 Differentiated Lessons		
In this series of lessons, students are working on the concept of tape/bar modeling multiplication and division word problems. They are developing this concept through concrete activities, pictorial activities and abstract activities. Everybody should do the cycle. Some students progress through it more quickly than others. Here are some things to think about as you do these lessons.		
Emergent	**On Grade Level**	**Above Grade Level**
Students need to understand one step problems. Make sure that students understand the idea of problem solving, solving one way and checking another. Make sure that you as the teacher have scaffolded the problems.	Students should be comfortable with tape/bar diagrams by 4th grade. This is not always the case and so it is important that the teacher scaffold the use of these models. So do lots of this work where students are modeling it and explaining it.	Extend the number range.

 Looking for Misunderstandings and Common Errors

Students have trouble with learning to represent their work with tape/bar diagrams. They need to take their time and use various models to act out and model the problems.

Figure 6.19 Anchor Chart

Solving Multiplication Word Problems with Tape Diagrams

Jane has 9 rings. She has 3 times as many as her sister. How many does her sister have?

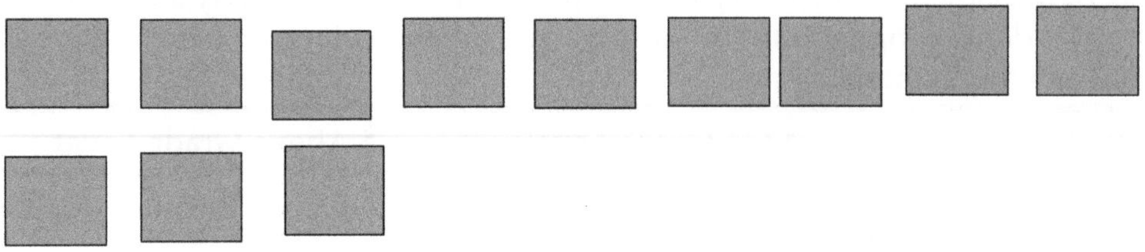

Sketch

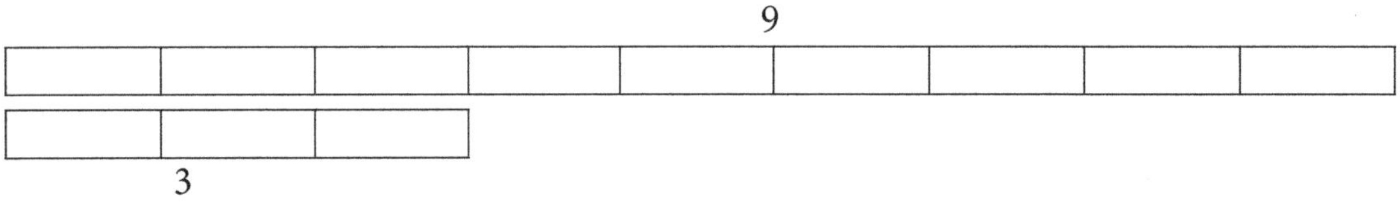

9

3

Concrete Lesson

Figure 6.20 Introduction

Introduction to Concrete Explorations	
Launch	**Teacher:** Today we are going to work on word problems. **Vocabulary:** Product Factor Multiply, Divisor, Dividend, Quotient, Compare, as many as, **Math Talk:** The answer is … My model is….
Model	**Teacher:** Luke had 4 marbles. He had 2 times as many as his brother. How many did his brother have? **Lucy:** Ted and I put 4 on top. It said he had 2 times as much as his brother. So his brother only has 2. ▢ ▢ ▢ ▢ ▢ ▢ **Teacher:** Dan had 6 marbles. He had 3 times as many as his brother. How many did his brother have?
Checking for Understanding	**Sasha:** Carlos and me made 1 row of 6. **Carlos:** His brother has 2. We divided the 6 into 3 groups. His brother has one of those groups. ▢ ▢ ▢ ▢ ▢ ▢ ▢ ▢ **Teacher:** Ok. I am going to give each one of you your own problem. I want you to read it. Solve it. Be ready to share how you did it. I am going to watch you and if you need help, look at our anchor charts, ask a friend or me.

Figure 6.21 Student Activity

	Concrete Student Activity
Guided Practice/ Checking for Understanding	The teacher passes out the problems. Students pull a card and act out their problems. The students each get a chance to share their problem and explain how they solved it. **Timmy:** My problem is this: The bakery had 8 chocolate chip cookies. They had 2 times as many chocolate chip cookies as lemon cookies. How many lemon cookies did they have? **Timmy:** So I put 8 cookies and divided them into 2 groups. 1 of those groups is the lemon group.
Set up for Independent Practice	Every child shares out their problem and how they solved it on the Array mat. We are going to be talking more about this in the upcoming days. Are there any questions? What was interesting today? What was tricky?

Figure 6.22 Lesson Close

Close
• What did we do today? • What was the math we were practicing? • What were we doing with our number tiles? • Was this easy or tricky? • Turn to a partner and state one thing you learned today.

Figure 6.23 Multiplication Comparison Cards

The bakery had 4 lemon cookies. They had twice as many lemon cookies as vanilla cookies. How many vanilla cookies did they have?	The bakery had 6 vanilla cookies. They had 2 times as many vanilla cookies as lemon cookies. How many vanilla cookies did they have?
The bakery had 6 lemon pies. They had 3 times as many lemon pies as chocolate pies. How many chocolate pies did they have?	The bakery had 9 chocolate cakes. They had 3 times as many chocolate cakes as lemon cakes. How many lemon cakes did they have?
The bakery had 10 lemon pies. They had 5 times as many lemon pies as chocolate pies. How many chocolate pies did they have?	The bakery had 8 chocolate cakes. They had 4 times as many chocolate cakes as lemon cakes. How many lemon cakes did they have?

Visual Lesson

Figure 6.24 Visual Introduction

	Introduction to Visual Explorations

Launch	**Teacher:** Today we are going to continue to work on solving word problems and modeling them with a tape diagram.
	
	Vocabulary: multiplication, word problem, product, factor, dividend, quotient, divisor
	
	Math Talk:
	  My strategy was…
	  My model was …

Model	The bakery had 6 chocolate muffins. They had 2 times as many chocolate muffins as lemon ones. How many lemon muffins did they have? **Teacher:** How could we model this problem with a tape diagram? **Don:** I drew 6 on the top and then 2 times as many would be 3 lemon ones. **Teacher:** Does everybody see this model? Who can explain it? Are the numbers in the right place? **Grace:** Yes. 3×2 would be 6.
Checking for Understanding	This conversation continues with the students using tape diagrams to model their stories.

Figure 6.25 Student Activity

Student Activity	
Guided Practice/ Checking for Understanding	The teacher passes out word problem cards. Students pull a card and model their problems. The students each get a chance to share their problem and explain how they solved it. **Maria: My problem is this:** The bakery had 4 chocolate pies. They had 2 times as many chocolate pies as lemon pies. How many lemon pies did they have? **Maria:** Here is my model. **Teacher:** Does everybody see that? You all are doing really well modeling with the tape diagram.
Set up for Independent Practice	*Teacher gives everybody a chance to do and discuss a problem. After everyone has shared the lesson ends.* "We are going to be talking more about this in the upcoming days. Are there any questions? What was interesting today? What was tricky?"

Figure 6.26 Lesson Close

Close
♦ What did we do today? ♦ What was the math we were practicing? ♦ What were we doing with our tape diagrams? ♦ Was this easy or tricky? ♦ Turn to a partner and state one thing you learned today.

Figure 6.27 Tape Diagram Cards

Brian had 6 marbles. He had 2 times as many as his brother. How many did his brother have?	Jamal had 9 marbles. He had 3 times as many as his brother. How many did his brother have?
Hong had 8 marbles. He had 4 times as many as his brother. How many did his brother have?	Jane had 10 marbles. She had 5 times as many as her brother. How many did her brother have?
Betty had 12 marbles. She had 2 times as many as her brother. How many did her brother have?	Jamila had 14 marbles. She had 2 times as many as her brother. How many did her brother have?
Barbara had 10 marbles. She had 2 times as many as her brother. How many did her brother have?	Grace had 8 marbles. She had 2 times as many as her brother. How many did her brother have?

Abstract Lesson

Figure 6.28 Abstract Introduction

	Introduction to Abstract Explorations

Launch	**Teacher:** Today we are going to play a word problem match game. You will match the problem, the tape diagram and the equation. **Vocabulary:** part-part whole, whole, part, word problem, count up, number sentence (equation)
	
	Math Talk: The whole is _____.
	         One part is _____.
	         The other part is _____.

Model	**Teacher:** Today we are going to play a match game. We have to find the word problem, the diagram and the number sentence that all match. There are 3 problems that are all mixed up in the bags. I am going to let you work with your partner to talk and discuss the problems and match them up. I am going to listen and ask you questions. Let's do 1 together. <table><tr><td>10</td><td rowspan="3">There were 10 big marbles and 5 small ones. How many times as many big marbles were there than small marbles?</td></tr><tr><td>5</td></tr><tr><td>$10 \div 5 = 2$ $2 \times 5 = 10$</td></tr></table>
Checking for Understanding	**Teacher:** Does everybody see this model. Who can explain it? **Ted:** 10 big and half of ten is 2. There are 2 times as many big marbles as small marbles. **Teacher:** I will be watching you discuss the problems with your partners. Be sure you are sure because I am going to definitely ask you questions about the matches you make.

Figure 6.29 Student Activity

Student Activity	
Guided Practice/ Checking for Understanding	The teacher watches the students as they work together to discuss and match the problems. **Teacher watches Leah and Tom.** How do you know this equation goes with the problem? **Leah:** Well I think what times 2 makes 4. It's 2. So Luke had 2 times as many as his brother. 4 2 $4 \div 2 = 2$ $2 \times 2 = 4$ Luke had 4 toy trucks. His brother had 2 toy trucks. How many times as many toy trucks did Luke have as his brother?
Set up for Independent Practice	The teacher continues to watch the groups as they work on matching their problems. When everyone has finished the teacher asks the students to explain their thinking. She also asks them what was easy and what was tricky.

Figure 6.30 Lesson Close

Close
♦ What did we do today? ♦ What was the math we were practicing? ♦ What were we doing with our word problems, tape diagrams and equations? ♦ Was this easy or tricky? ♦ Turn to a partner and state one thing you learned today.

Figure 6.31 Word Problem Cards

10 2 $10 \div 2 = 5$ $2 \times 5 = 10$	Jamal had 10 toy trucks. His brother had 2 toy trucks. How many times as many toy trucks did Jamal have as his brother?
8 2 $8 \div 2 = 4$ $2 \times 4 = 10$	Hong had 8 toy trucks. His brother had 2 toy trucks. How many times as many toy trucks did Hong have as his brother?
10 2 $10 \div 5 = 2$ $5 \times 2 = 10$	Marta had 10 marbles. Her brother had 5 marbles. How many times as many marbles did Marta have as her brother?

Section Summary

In this section we have talked about solving multiplication comparison problems with a focus on using tiles and tape diagrams. In most state standards, students should be introduced to tape diagrams in the second grade. Sometimes, this doesn't happen. In either case, it is good to start with 1-inch tiles as the scaffold for doing this concretely and then drawing out what they did on 1-inch tile paper. They could also use Cuisenaire ᵗᵐ rods to do this. The next step is to have the students draw what they built. This cycle of concrete, pictorial to abstract is a great cycle to build student confidence about being able to model their thinking with tape diagrams.

Elapsed Time Word Problems

Overview

Figure 6.32 Overview

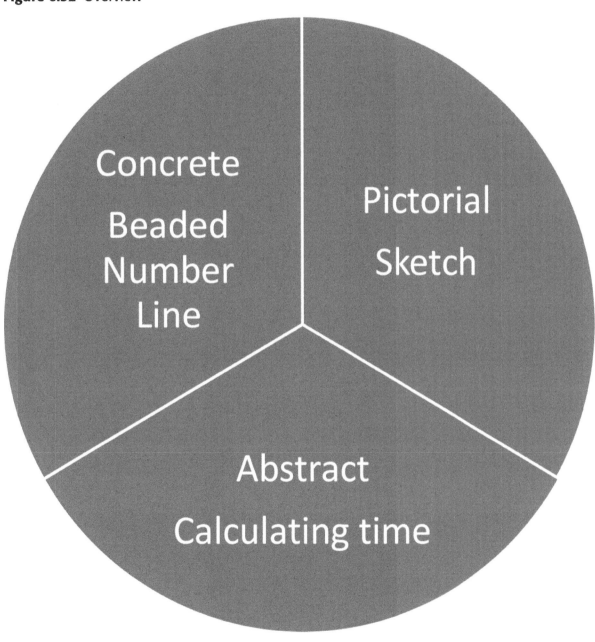

Figure 6.33 Planning Template

Elapsed Time Word Problems

Big Idea: There are different types of elapsed time word problems. The big idea is for students to understand how we measure time. **Enduring Understanding**: We can model problems in many ways. **Essential Question**: What are the ways to model elapsed time problems? **I can statement**: I can model elapsed time word problems.	**Materials** ♦ Tools: Elapsed Time Rulers ♦ Templates: Clock Templates; Open Number lines ♦ Elapsed Time Cards ♦ Crayons

Cycle of Engagement

Concrete:

Pictorial: Drawing

Abstract

3:25 to 4:10

3:25 to 4 is 35 min.

35 min + 10 min.

45 min.

Vocabulary & Language Frames

♦ Count Up
♦ Count Back
♦ Minutes
♦ Hours
♦ Hands
♦ Start time
♦ End time
♦ Elapsed Time

Figure 6.34 Differentiation

3 Differentiated Lessons		
In this series of lessons, students are working on elapsed time problems. They are developing this concept through concrete activities, pictorial activities and abstract activities. Everybody should do the cycle. Some students progress through it more quickly than others. Here are some things to think about as you do these lessons.		
Below Grade Level	**On Grade Level**	**Above Grade Level**
Review adding and subtracting. As you introduce this to students, do a lot of work by modeling it in different ways.	Students work with a clock and also a number line.	Extend the number range telling time across hours.

 Looking for Misunderstandings and Common Errors

Elapsed time problems are tricky. I like to teach them with the cubes going around so the students can physically count the minutes first. Then I like to do it with an illustrated clock before they move onto a number line diagram.

Figure 6.35 Anchor Chart

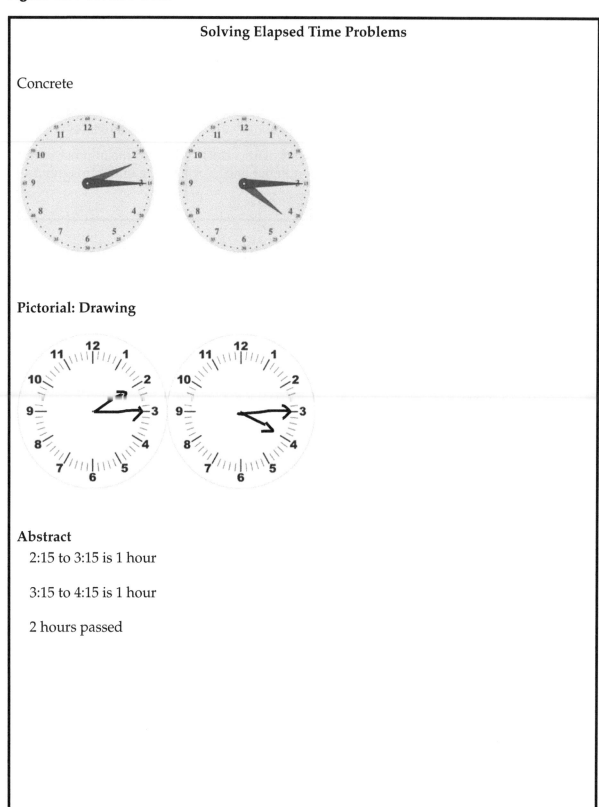

Solving Elapsed Time Problems

Concrete

Pictorial: Drawing

Abstract

2:15 to 3:15 is 1 hour

3:15 to 4:15 is 1 hour

2 hours passed

Concrete Lesson

Figure 6.36 Concrete Introduction

	Introduction to Concrete Explorations
Launch	Teacher: Today we are going to work on telling time problems. We are going to use our virtual clocks to scaffold our thinking. You can use it as a tool if you would like too. Vocabulary: elapsed time Minutes Hours Ruler measure Math Talk: ____ minutes passed.
Model	Students pull up virtual clocks on their devices. Teacher: Let's use our clocks to think about these problems. *Lucy left her house. She was gone for and 45 minutes. When could she have left and when could she have come back?* **Miles:** She could have left at 1:00 and came back at 1:45. **Tami:** She could have left 12:20 and came back at 1:05.
Checking for Understanding	**Teacher:** Listen to this problem. *Kiyana left her house and came back 35 minutes later. What time could she have left and what time could she have come back?* **Katie:** She could have left at 6:15 and come back at 6:50. **Teacher:** Ok. Does everybody understand what Katie did? Does it make sense? **Teacher:** Ok. I am going to give each one of you your own problem. I want you to read it. Solve it. Be ready to share how you did it. I am going to watch you and if you need help, look at our anchor charts and of course you can ask me.

Figure 6.37 Student Activity

<table>
<tr><th colspan="2" align="center">Student Activity</th></tr>
<tr><td>Guided Practice/
Checking for
Understanding</td><td>The teacher passes out the problems. Students pull a card and act out their problems with virtual clocks. The students each get a chance to share their problem and explain how they solved it.

Teacher: Remy explain your thinking to us.

Remy: My problem was: *Leti left her house for 35 minutes. When could she have left and when could she have come back?* I picked 4:30. So 35 more minutes would be 5:05.</td></tr>
<tr><td>Set up for
Independent
Practice</td><td>Every child shares out their problem and how they solved it on the virtual clocks. We are going to be talking more about that in the upcoming days. Are there any questions? What was interesting today? What was tricky?</td></tr>
</table>

Figure 6.38 Lesson Close

<table>
<tr><th align="center">Close</th></tr>
<tr><td>◆ What did we do today?
◆ What was the math we were practicing?
◆ What were we doing with our clock templates?
◆ Was this easy or tricky?
◆ Turn to a partner and state one thing you learned today.</td></tr>
</table>

Figure 6.39 Word Problem Cards

Kelly left her house for 30 minutes. When could she have left and when can she have come back?	Grace left her house for 45 minutes. When could she have left and when can she have come back?
Marta left her house for 20 minutes. When could she have left and when can she have come back?	Jamila left her house for 65 minutes. When could she have left and when can she have come back?
Hong left his house for 48 minutes. When could he have left and when can he have come back?	Jamal left his house for 59 minutes. When could he have left and when can he have come back?

Figure 6.40 Visual Introduction

Introduction to Visual Explorations	
Launch	**Teacher:** Today we are going to work more on elapsed time problems. We are going to use a clock to look at the elapsed **Vocabulary: elapsed time, ruler, minutes, hours, hands,** **Teacher: Let's look at this clock.**
Model	**Teacher:** Here is the problem: Melissa arrived at the cinema at 6:34. She had left her house 25 minutes earlier. What time did she leave her house? **Tom:** We could count backwards from 4:34. **Marta:** We could also just subtract 29 minutes from 34 minutes. **Teacher:** Yes, could you model it with the clock too? **Jose:** Yes, start at 34 and count back 29 minutes.
Checking for Understanding	**Teacher:** Excellent work. How do you know you are correct? **Tom:** We could subtract to double check. **Teacher:** Yes we could do that too. Today I am going to let you each pick problems and solve them with a partner and then share your thinking with the group.

Figure 6.41 Student Activity

Visual Student Activity

The teacher passes out word problem cards. Students pull a card and tell their problems. The students each get a chance to share their problem and explain how they solved it. This time they don't build it first. They model it with clocks only

Maria: Our problem was this:

> **Part 1: Masey arrived to her grandma's at 4:35. She left 17 minutes earlier? What time did she leave to go to her grandma's house?**
>
>
>
> **Way 1 with a model:** We counted back from 4:35.
> **Way 2 with numbers:** We subtracted 17 from 35.

Teacher gives everybody a chance to do and discuss a problem. After everyone has shared the lesson ends.
We are going to be talking more about this in the upcoming days. Are there any questions? What was interesting today? What was tricky?

Figure 6.42 Elapsed Time Word Problem Cards

Larry got to school at 8:45. He left his house 1 hour and 15 minutes before. What time did he leave his house?

Way 1: Clock Model

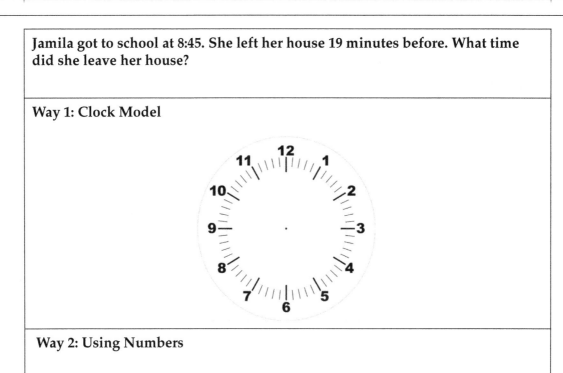

Way 2: Using Numbers

Jamila got to school at 8:45. She left her house 19 minutes before. What time did she leave her house?

Way 1: Clock Model

Way 2: Using Numbers

Figure 6.42 (Continued)

Marta got to school at 8:45. She left her house 1 hour and 25 minutes before. What time did she leave her house?

Way 1: Clock Model

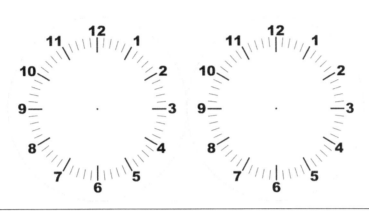

Way 2: Using Numbers

Hong got to school at 8:45. He left his house 39 minutes before. What time did he leave his house?

Way 1: Clock Model

Way 2: Using Numbers

Figure 6.42 (Continued)

Tina left her house at _____. She came back by _____. How long was she gone?

Way 1: Clock Model

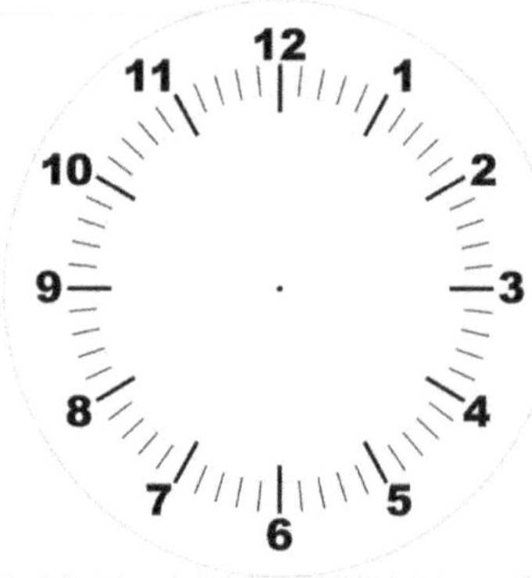

Way 2: Using Numbers

Miguel left his house at _____. He came back by _____. How long was he gone?

Way 1: Clock Model

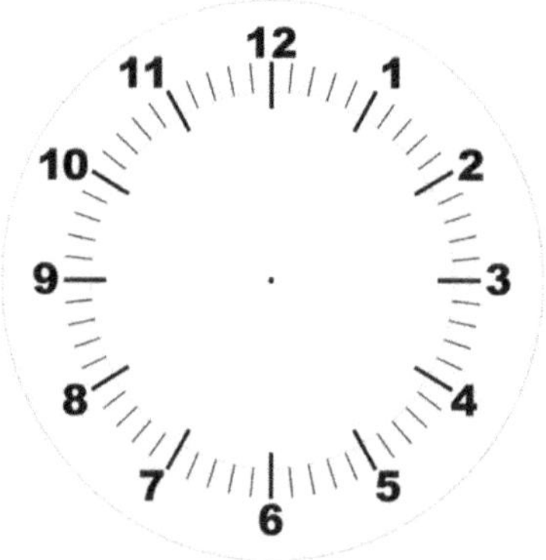

Way 2: Using Numbers

Figure 6.43 Lesson Close

Close
◆ What did we do today?   ◆ What was the math we were practicing?   ◆ What were we doing with our clocks?   ◆ Was this easy or tricky?   ◆ Turn to a partner and state one thing you learned today.

Abstract Lesson

Figure 6.44 Abstract Introduction

Introduction to Abstract Activities

Launch	**Teacher:** Today we are going to continue to work solving elapsed time problems. Let's look at our math talk chart: **Vocabulary: take away, subtract, minus sign, plus sign, altogether, addend, compare, more than, fewer than, equation model** **Math Talk:** **This was my strategy....**
Model	**Teacher:** Marta left her house at 3:45. She came back at 5:25. How long was she gone? Let's think about this together. How could we model the elapsed time on our number line? 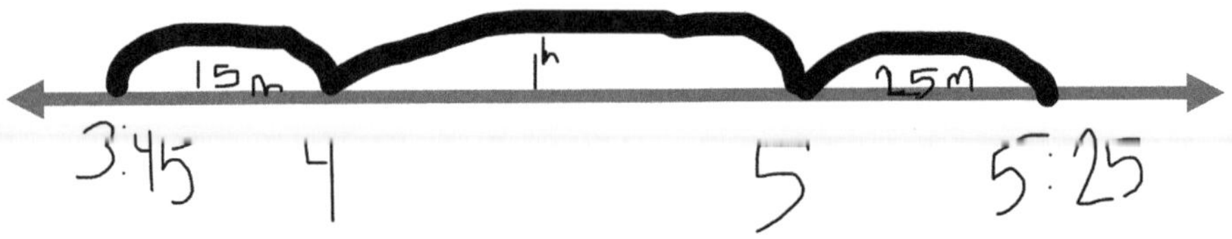 **Jay-Jay:** I jumped 15 min. to 4 and then an hour to 5 and then 25 more min. 25 and 15 is 40 + 1... so she was gone for an hour and 40 min.
Checking for Understanding	**Teacher:** Who did it another way? **Ted:** I jumped from 3:45 to 4:45 and then I jumped a half hour to 5:15 and then 10 min more. 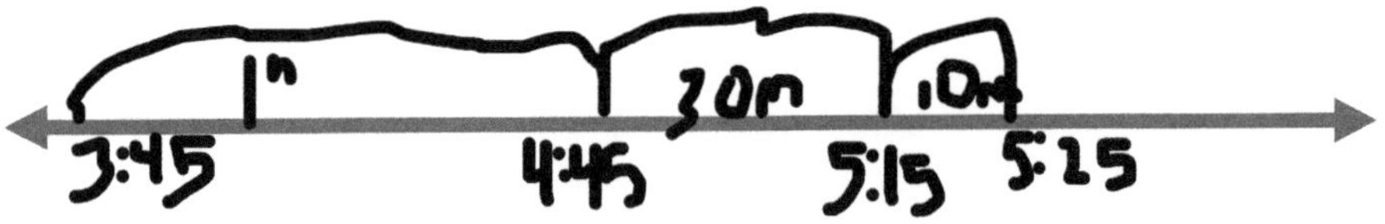 **Teacher:** Ok, so just like with the open number line, we can jump different ways? I am going to give each one of you your own problem and I want you to read your problem and then decide which way you are going to model your problem. Each person is going to get a chance to do one and explain their thinking.

Figure 6.45 Student Activity

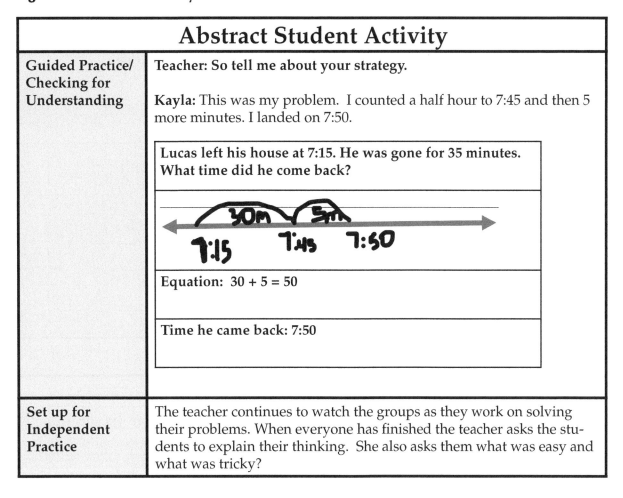

Guided Practice/ Checking for Understanding	**Teacher: So tell me about your strategy.** **Kayla:** This was my problem. I counted a half hour to 7:45 and then 5 more minutes. I landed on 7:50. **Lucas left his house at 7:15. He was gone for 35 minutes. What time did he come back?** 30m / 5m 7:15 7:45 7:50 **Equation: 30 + 5 = 50** **Time he came back: 7:50**
Set up for Independent Practice	The teacher continues to watch the groups as they work on solving their problems. When everyone has finished the teacher asks the students to explain their thinking. She also asks them what was easy and what was tricky?

Figure 6.46 Lesson Close

Close
◆ What did we do today? ◆ What was the math we were practicing? ◆ What were we doing with our open number lines? ◆ Was this easy or tricky? ◆ Turn to a partner and state one thing you learned today.

Figure 6.47 Word Problem Cards

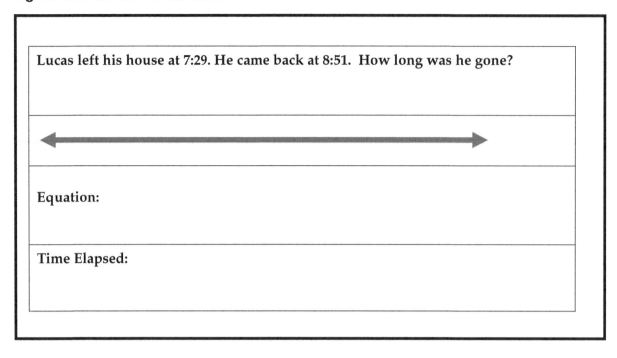

Lucas left his house at 7:29. He came back at 8:51. How long was he gone?

Equation:

Time Elapsed:

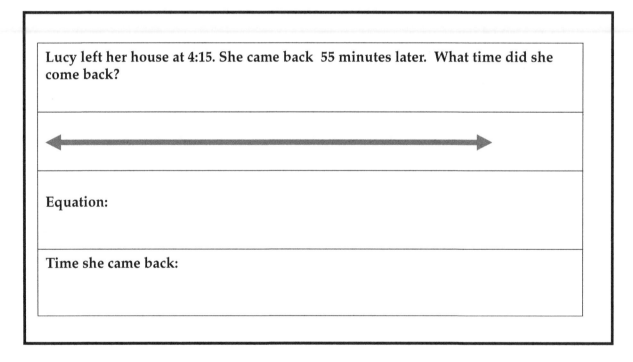

Lucy left her house at 4:15. She came back 55 minutes later. What time did she come back?

Equation:

Time she came back:

Figure 6.47 (Continued)

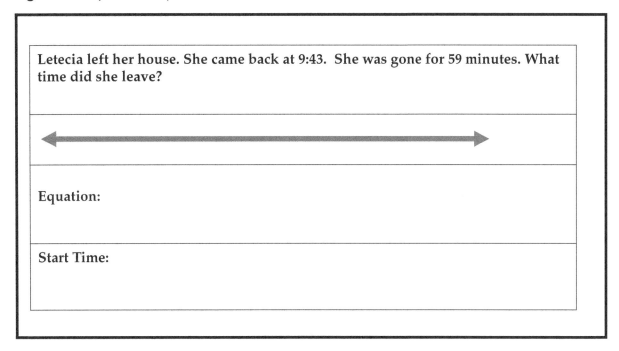

Letecia left her house. She came back at 9:43. She was gone for 59 minutes. What time did she leave?

Equation:

Start Time:

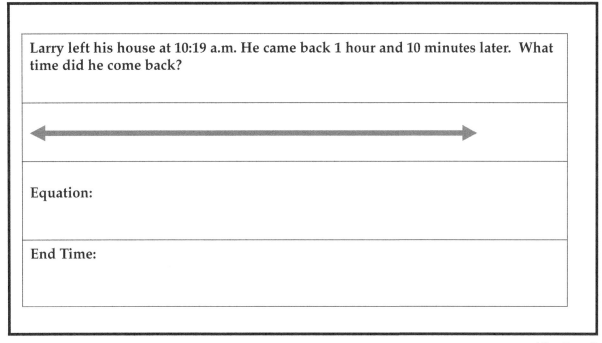

Larry left his house at 10:19 a.m. He came back 1 hour and 10 minutes later. What time did he come back?

Equation:

End Time:

(Continued)

Figure 6.47 (Continued)

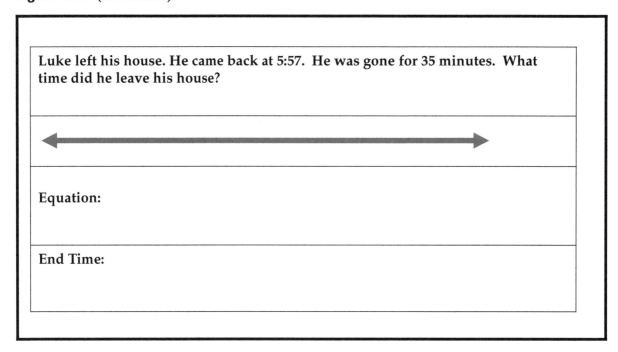

Luke left his house. He came back at 5:57. He was gone for 35 minutes. What time did he leave his house?

Equation:

End Time:

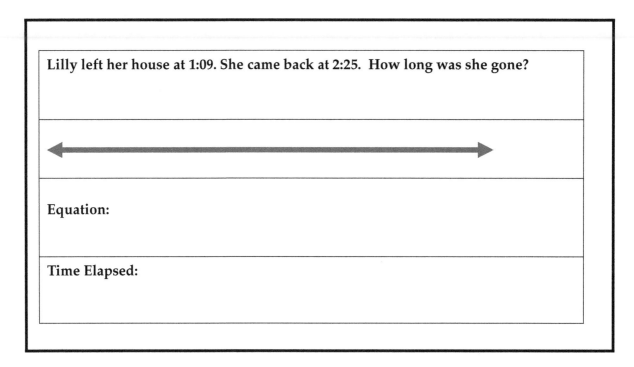

Lilly left her house at 1:09. She came back at 2:25. How long was she gone?

Equation:

Time Elapsed:

Section Summary

Students have a great deal of trouble with elapsed time problems. Using various scaffolds up until they can draw a number line diagram to solve the problems takes time. Small groups are a great space to explore modeling these problems in different ways. In this section we looked at the different types of elapsed time problems. It is important to work on all the different types of problems and to have students explain their strategies for solving them.

3 Read Problems

Figure 6.48 3 Read Problems Planning Template

3 Read Problems

Big Idea: We can use different strategies and models to solve word problems. **Enduring Understanding:** Students will understand how to model problems in many ways. **Essential Question:** What are the ways to model this type of problem? **I can statement:** I can use tools to model my thinking.	**Materials** ♦ Problem Solving Mats ♦ Cards ♦ Crayons
Cycle of Engagement Concrete-Pictorial-Abstract In this type of problem, the class chorally reads the problem 3 times. The first time the class reads the problem, they focus on what is happening in the problem. The second time they focus on what the numbers mean. The third time they focus on asking questions about the problems.	**Vocabulary & Language Frames** ♦ Strategies ♦ Modelo ♦ Tools **Math Talk** My strategy was… My model was… **Mathematical Processes/Practices** ♦ Problem Solving ♦ Reasoning ♦ Modeling ♦ Tools

Figure 6.49 3 Read Word Problems Anchor Chart

---

3 Read Word Problem

We can read a problem 3 times.

The first time we read it and think about the situation.
   What is the story about? Who is in it? What is happening?

The second time we read it and think about the numbers.
   What are the numbers? What do they mean? What might we do with those numbers in this situation?

The third time we read it and think about what questions we could ask.
   What do we notice in this story? What do we wonder? What do we want to ask about this story?

   The Jones family went on vacation. They drove 229 miles on Monday. They drove 325 miles on Tuesday. They drove 99 miles on Wednesday.

First Read: What is this story about? It is about a family who went on vacation.

Second Read: What do the numbers mean? They tell us how far they drove. On Monday they drove 229 miles. On Tuesday they drove 325 miles and on Wednesday they drove 99 miles.

Third Read: What could we ask about this story?

How far did they drive altogether?
How much farther did they drive on Monday than on Wednesday?
How many fewer miles did they drive on Wednesday than they drove on Tuesday?

Figure 6.50 3 Read Word Problems Lesson

	3 Read Word Problems Lesson
Launch	**Teacher:** Today we are going to work on word problems. We are going to do a 3 read, like the ones we do in whole group. **Vocabulary: model, strategy,** **Math Talk:** ♦ My strategy was… ♦ My **model was…**
Model	*Story: The bakery made several cookies. They made 306 chocolate chip, 278 peanut butter and 224 lemon ones.* *First Read: What is this story about?* *It is about the bakery. They have 3 different types of cookies.* *Second Read: What do the numbers mean?* *They have 306 chocolate chip cookies, 278 peanut butter cookies and 224 lemon ones.* *Third Read: What could we ask about this story?* *How many cookies were there altogether?* *How many more chocolate chip cookies did they have than peanut butter ones?* *How many fewer lemon cookies do they have than chocolate chip cookies?*
Checking for Understanding	*Teacher: Ok, pick 2 questions and answer them. We will come back in a few minutes to discuss them…. Who answered question 1? Tell us your strategy and show us a model of your thinking.*

Figure 6.50 (Continued)

Guided Practice/ Checking for Understanding	*Timothy: I did how many do they have altogether? I modeled it in a part-part whole diagram. My strategy was to add the hundreds and then the tens and then the ones.*
	 | ? | | 306 | 278 | 224 | *300 + 200 + 200 = 700* *0 + 70 + 20 = 90* *4 + 6 + 8 = 18* *700 + 90 + 18 = 808* *Teacher: Ok, who did question 2?* *Eric: I did how many more chocolate chip cookies than peanut butter ones. 306 − 278. So I counted up, I like doing that. From 278 it's 22 to 300 and the 6 more…so that is 28.*
Set up for Independent Practice	*Students continue to share their thinking with the group. When they are done the teacher facilitates a conversation about what the math was for the day and then what students thought was easy and what they thought was tricky.*

Figure 6.51 Lesson Close

Close
♦ What did we do today? ♦ What was the math we were practicing? ♦ Was this easy or tricky? ♦ Turn to a partner and state one thing you learned today.

Figure 6.52 3 Read Cards

The teacher had 85 pencils. 45 were blue and 24 were green and the rest were yellow.	Terri biked 3 miles for 3 days. Mary biked 4 miles for 4 days.
Marta had 96 red marbles, 59 orange marbles and 25 blue marbles.	The store had 205 red apples, 42 green apples and 159 yellow apples.
The jewelry store had 279 gold rings and 325 silver rings.	Grandma made fruit punch. She used 450 ml of apple juice, 150 ml of orange juice and 350 ml of pineapple juice.
The bakery had 5 boxes of chocolate cupcakes with 2 cupcakes in each box. It also had 3 boxes of lemon cupcakes with 4 in each box.	The toy store had 800 marbles. They had 429 rainbow marbles, they had 308 jumbo marbles and the rest were mini marbles.

Picture Prompt Word Problems

Figure 6.53 Picture Prompt Word Problems Planning Template

Picture Prompt Word Problems

Big Idea: Word problems are a part of our everyday lives. **Enduring Understanding:** Students will understand that they can model problems in many ways. There are also many different strategies to solve them. **Essential Question:** Where do we see word problems in real life? **I can statement:** I can model problems.	**Materials** ♦ Tools: Manipulatives ♦ Templates ♦ Cards ♦ Crayons
	Questions ♦ What is your strategy? ♦ What is your model? ♦ Why does that work? ♦ How can you show that?
Cycle of Engagement **Concrete:** **Pictorial: Drawing** **Pictorial: Drawing** **Abstract: Equations** $2 + m = 6$ $2 + 4 = 6$	**Vocabulary & Language Frames** Add, subtract, take away, sum, difference My strategy was … My model was …
	Math Processes/Practices ♦ Problem Solving ♦ Reasoning ♦ Models ♦ Tools

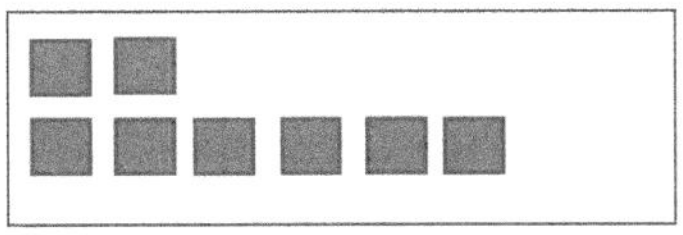

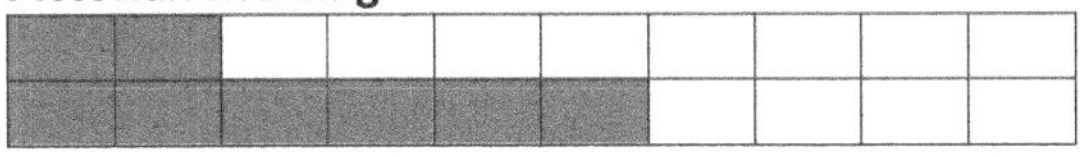

Figure 6.54 Picture Prompt Word Lesson

Picture Prompt Word Problems Lesson

Launch	**Teacher:** Today we are going to work on word problems. We are going to do a picture prompt word problems today.
	Vocabulary: model, strategy,
	Math Talk: ◆ My strategy was… ◆ My model was…
Model	**Teacher:** Today we are going to look at pictures and tell word problems. Let's think about some word problems for this picture.  **Luke:** The candy bar had 4 rows and 7 columns. How many pieces of candy can you get? **Teacher:** Ok, that works! What's the product? **Marta:** 28 pieces.
Checking for Understanding	**Ted:** You could say: Kelly gave her sister 2 rows of her candy bar. How many pieces did she get? **Kelly:** 2×7 is 14 pieces.

Figure 6.54 (Continued)

Guided Practice/ Checking for Understanding	**Teacher:** Who has another one, maybe 2-step?
	Claire: Luke gave his brother 4 pieces of the candy bar, he gave his sister 2 times as much. How many pieces did give away altogether? How many pieces did he have left?
	Dan: He gave away 4 pieces and 8 pieces. Altogether he gave away 12 pieces and he has 16 left.
Set up for Independent Practice	**Teacher:** Ok. Who's next? The teacher goes around the circle and everyone gets a chance to share their stories. They then wrap up and go to workstations.

Figure 6.55 Open Word Problems

	Open Word Problems Lesson
Launch	**Teacher:** Today we are going to work on word problems. **Vocabulary:** model, strategy, tool, sum, difference, addend, **Math Talk:** My strategy was… My model was…
Model	**Teacher:** The answer is 16 strawberries. What is the question? (Tell a multiplication or division word problem). **Terry:** I know. There were 4 baskets and in each basket there were 4 strawberries. How many strawberries are there? **Kayla:** I could say there were 1 basket and 16 strawberries in each basket. **Teacher:** Absolutely. All of these work. Can you both draw a model of what you said?
Checking for Understanding	**Teacher:** Who can think of a division one with this quotient? **Kayla:** Ok, I got one. Maite had a box of 32 strawberries. She shared it with her sister. How many did each person get? **Maite:** 16 **Joe:** It's hard to think of division problems with 16 as the quotient. **Teacher:** What might help us? (Students think out loud)….

Figure 6.55 (Continued)

Guided Practice/ Checking for Understanding	Let's think about how a table might help. How are multiplication and division related?
	$2 \times 16 = 32$
	$3 \times 16 = 48$
	$4 \times 16 = 64$
	$5 \times 16 = 80$
	Taylor: Well like we could say there were 48 strawberries and they were put into 3 boxes. How many were in each box?
Set up for Independent Practice	*The students continue telling stories.. They focus on looking at the pattern. After they finish, the teacher asks them what they were doing and if it was easy or tricky. Then, the students are released back to continue their menu work.*

Section Summary

It is important to do open questions with students where they have to contextualize numbers. This is part of the mathematical practices and processes (CCSSM, 2010). We want students to be able to reason about numbers. Students should be encouraged to think about different problem situations concretely, pictorially and abstractly. We want students to be able to tell stories, not only solve them. Giving them rich structures to do that is vital.

Depth of Knowledge

Depth of Knowledge is a framework that encourages us to ask questions that require that students think, reason, explain, defend and justify their thinking (Webb, 2002). Here is snapshot of what that can look like in terms of place value work (see Figures 6.56 and 6.57).

Figure 6.56 DOK Activities

	What are different strategies and models that we can use to solve measurement problems.	What are different strategies and models to model multiplication comparison problems with tiles and tape diagrams.	What are different strategies and models that we can use to solve elapsed time problems.
Dok Level 1 (these are questions where students are required to simply recall/reproduce an answer/do a procedure)	Solve. Write a set-up equation (with a symbol for the unknown) and a solution equation. Grandma used 540 ml of apple juice, 668 ml of orange juice and 599 ml of pineapple juice, in her fruit punch. How much fruit punch did she make altogether in liters?	Solve with manipulatives. Write the equation. The bakery had a display of donuts. They had 10 lemon donuts and 2 times as many chocolate donuts. How many chocolate donuts did they have?	Sue left her house at 3:10. She came back at 5:55. How long was she gone?
Dok Level 2 (these are questions where students have to use information, think about concepts and reason) This is considered a more challenging problem than a level 1 problem.	Solve and model in two different ways. Explain your thinking. Grandma made 2 liters of fruit punch. She used 340 ml of apple juice, 267 ml of orange juice and the rest was pineapple juice. How much orange juice did she use?	Solve with a math sketch. Explain your thinking. Write a multiplication comparison word problem using the numbers where you are looking for the bigger part.	Solve the problem with a model and an equation. Sue left her house at _____. She came back at _____. How long was she gone?
Dok Level 3 (these are questions where students have to reason, plan, explain, justify and defend their thinking)	Solve. Grandma made some fruit punch. She used apple, orange and pineapple juice. She made 1 liter of punch altogether. What are some possible combinations of the juice that she could have made? Defend your answer. Prove that it is correct by solving one way and checking another.	Solve. The answer is 12. Write a multiplicative comparison problem. Defend your answer. Prove that it is correct by solving one way and checking another.	Marcus was gone for 1 hour and 25 minutes. When could he have left and when could he have come back? Make up a problem and solve it on the number line. Defend your thinking. Prove that you are correct.

Also, Robert Kaplinsky has done a great job in pushing our thinking forward with the Depth of Knowledge Matrices he created. (https://robertkaplinsky.com/depth-knowledge-matrix-elementary-math/). The Kentucky Department of Education (2007) has a great document illustrating DOK Matrices.

A great resource for asking open questions is Marion Small's *Good Questions: Great ways to differentiate mathematics instruction in the standards-based classroom* (2017).

Figure 6.57 Asking Rigorous Questions

Dok 1	Dok 2 At this level students explain their thinking.	Dok 3 At this level students have to justify, defend and prove their thinking with objects, drawings and diagrams.
What is the answer to ??? Can you model the problem? Can you identify the answer that matches this equation?	How do you know that the equation is correct? Can you pick the correct answer and explain why it is correct? How can you model that problem in more than one way? What is another way to model that problem? Can you model that on the ....??? Give me an example of a ...type of problem.... Which answer is incorrect? Explain your thinking.	Can you prove that your answer is correct? Prove that... Explain why that is the answer... Show me how to solve that and explain what you are doing.

Key Points

♦ Measurement problems
♦ Modeling multiplication word problems
♦ Elapsed time word problems
♦ 3 read problems
♦ Picture prompts

Chapter Summary

It is important to work with students in small guided math groups focusing on word problems. Word problems have a learning trajectory (Carpenter et al., 1999/2015). Most states have outlined the word problem types that each grade level is responsible for in their standards. In a guided math group, the goal is to work with students around the word problem types that they are learning.

Students are usually at different levels when learning word problems. They are scaffolded into a hierarchy that goes from easy to challenging. By fourth grade, students dive deep into all of the nine types of multiplication and division word problems, as well as measurement problems. Measurement is often difficult for students, and that is why it is so important to give students an opportunity to work in small groups to experience the math and actually to do the measurements.

The small group discussion should reference the whole group problem solving work. The focus should be on getting students to think about the context and the numbers, to reason about the problem and use visual representations and tools to unpack it. Students should have to write an equation with a symbol for the unknown and solve one way and check another. Problem solving should be done throughout the year, in different parts of math workshop, during the introduction, in math workstations, sometimes in guided math groups and sometimes for homework.

Reflection Questions

1. How are you currently teaching word problem lessons?
2. Are you making sure that you do concrete, pictorial and abstract activities?
3. What do your students struggle with the most?
4. What ideas are you taking away from this chapter that might inform your work?

References

Carpenter, T. P., Fennema, E., Franke, M. L., Levi, L., & Empson, S. B. (2015). *Children's mathematics: Cognitively guided instruction.* NH: Heinemann.

Common Core State Standards Mathematical Practices. (2010). Retrieved January 15, 2021 from http://www.corestandards.org/Math/Practice/

Kentucky Department of Education. (2007). *Support materials for core content for assessment version 4.1 mathematics.* Retrieved January 15, 2017.

Schoenfeld, A. H. (1992). Learning to think mathematically: Problem solving, metacognition, and sense making in mathematics. In D. A. Grouws (Ed.), *Handbook of research on mathematics teaching and learning* (pp. 334–370). Reston, VA: National Council of Teachers of Mathematics.

Stacey, K., & MacGregor, M. (1999). Learning the algebraic method of solving problems. *The Journal of Mathematical Behavior*, 18(2), 149–167. https://doi.org/10.1016/S0732-3123(99)00026-7

Verschaffel, L., Greer, B., & De Corte, E. (2000). *Making sense of word problems.* Lisse, The Netherlands: Swets & Zeitlinger.

Webb, N. (2002). *An analysis of the alignment between mathematics standards and assessments for three states.* Paper presented at the annual meeting of the American Educational Research Association, New Orleans, LA.

7

Place Value Guided Math Lessons

The research clearly confirms that place value is very important (National Council of Teachers of Mathematics, 2000; Sherman, Richardson, & Yard, 2013). Researchers have found that a strong understanding of place value has a positive impact on later mathematics achievement (Miura, Okamato, Chungsoon, & Steere, 1993; Moeller, Pixner, Zuber, Kaufmann, & Nuerk, 2011).

Place value has a solid place in fourth grade. In this grade one of the things that you want to do is really continue working on the second grade and third grade standards so that students can become confident and proficient in the concepts that they will build on and then use extensively in fourth grade. Up to second grade, students learn about 17–18 topics and in third they usually learn three more topics.

In these lessons we explore how to build an understanding of place value along the learning trajectory so that students understand what it looks like, feels like and how to use it to understand and work with numbers. Students should have plenty of opportunities to practice the big ideas concretely, pictorially and abstractly. Students should have plenty of opportunities to use various tools to explore the concepts. These concepts are the foundation of our math system. Too often, students are rushed through a place value chapter and then the concepts are never addressed again. Place value should be interwoven throughout the year, and it should stay up as a workstation center. The National Council of Teachers of Mathematics (NCTM, 2000) notes that students should "use multiple models to develop initial understandings of place value and the base-ten number system."

I want to emphasize that not only should place value blocks be used but also rekenreks, beaded number lines, base ten paper and sketches. Cuisenaire rods and digiblocks™ are also great tools to use. The idea is that the more ways that students can think about and explore the concept, the more opportunities they have to own it and make sense of it. The research says that the more ways that students can model concepts the better their understanding. The sample guided math lessons in this chapter take the students through the cycle of concrete, pictorial and abstract to teach:

- ◆ Representing numbers in a variety of ways
- ◆ Rounding numbers
- ◆ Multiplying 2-digit numbers
- ◆ Dividing 2-digit numbers by 1-digit numbers

DOI: 10.4324/9781003169581-7

Research Note 🔍

- A good foundation in place value is essential (National Council of Teachers of Mathematics, 2000; National Research Council, 2009).
- Research consistently finds that students struggle with place and have difficulty understanding tens and ones (Hanich, Jordan, Kaplan, & Dick, 2001; Jordan & Hanich, 2000; Kamii, 1985; Kamii & Joseph, 1988).
- The National Council of Teachers of Mathematics (NCTM, 2000, in their Number and Operations Standards for Grades Pre-K-2) states students should "use multiple models to develop initial understandings of place value and the base-ten number system."

Exploring Representing Numbers

Overview

Figure 7.1 Overview

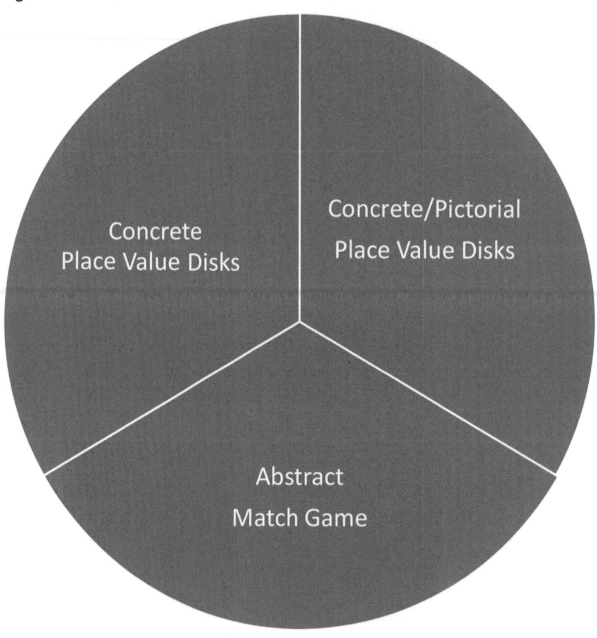

Concrete
Place Value Disks

Concrete/Pictorial
Place Value Disks

Abstract
Match Game

Figure 7.2 Planning Template

Representing Numbers in a Variety of Ways

Big Idea: Numbers, Base Ten System, Equivalence **Enduring Understanding:** Students will understand that our system is based on using the digits 0 to 9, groups of ten and place value. **Essential Question:** What are the ways to model hundreds, tens and ones? **I can statement:** I can break apart a number into hundreds, tens and ones.	**Materials** • Tools: Place value disks

Cycle of Engagement	Vocabulary & Language Frames
Concrete:  **Pictorial: Drawing**  **Abstract** 535 = 500 + 30 + 5	Vocabulary: add, sum, addend, plus, equals, makes, tens, ones, hundreds Math Talk: I have ____ hundreds and ___tens and ____ones. I have _____. **Math Processes/Practices** • Models • Tools • Structure • Patterns

Figure 7.3 Differentiation

3 Differentiated Lessons		
In this series of lessons, students are working on the concept of representing a number in a variety of ways. They are developing this concept through concrete activities, pictorial activities and abstract activities. Here are some things to think about as you do these lessons.		

Emerging	On Grade Level	Above Grade Level
Do a lot of work with students building the hundreds, tens and ones.	Work on representing numbers within 1 million.	Work with larger numbers.

 Looking for Misunderstandings and Common Errors

Students have trouble with the language of place value. Be sure to do activities and energizers where you unpack the language. For example, students will write two hundred five like this: 2005. So it is important to work with the actual place and value of numbers.

Figure 7.4 Anchor Chart

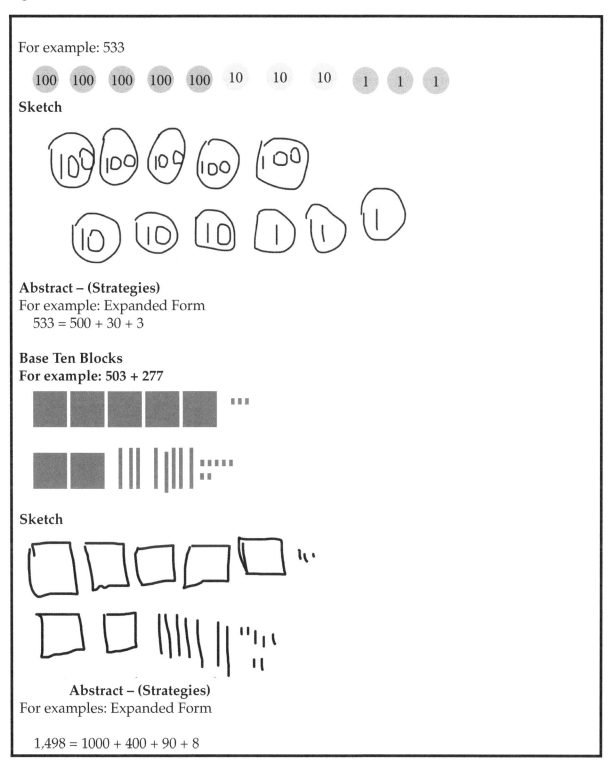

For example: 533

100 100 100 100 100 10 10 10 1 1 1

Sketch

Abstract – (Strategies)
For example: Expanded Form
533 = 500 + 30 + 3

Base Ten Blocks
For example: 503 + 277

Sketch

Abstract – (Strategies)
For examples: Expanded Form

1,498 = 1000 + 400 + 90 + 8

Concrete Lesson

Figure 7.5 Concrete Introduction

Introduction to Concrete Explorations

Launch	**Teacher:** Today we are going to work on looking at how to represent numbers in a variety of ways. We will be working with place value disks. **Vocabulary:** thousands, hundreds, tens, ones, place value, expanded form, number name **Math Talk:** _____ and ___ make _____
Model	**Teacher:** Today we are going to build numbers in different ways. We will be working with the place value disks. Everybody has their own bag of disks. Build the number 1, 745 any way you want. **Teacher:** Now build that same number but a different way. And then somebody explain your work. **Maite:** I did 1000 and 7 hundreds and 4 tens and 5 ones. The other way I did was 17 hundreds, 4 tens and 5 ones.
Checking for Understanding	**Teacher:** Ok, so I am going to give each one of you a problem to solve. I want you to solve it any way you want and then explain it back to the group. Model it with your virtual manipulatives.

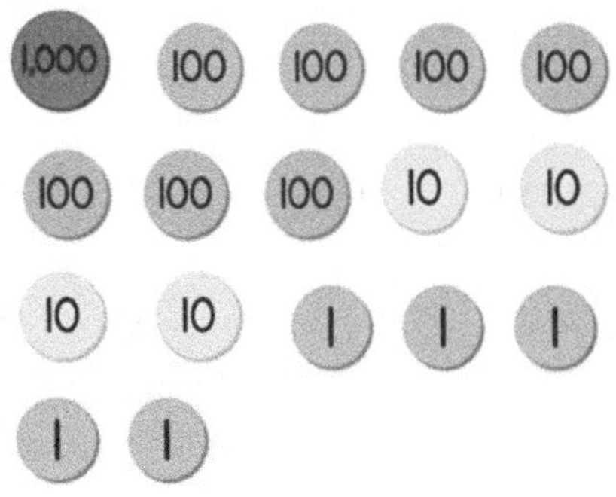

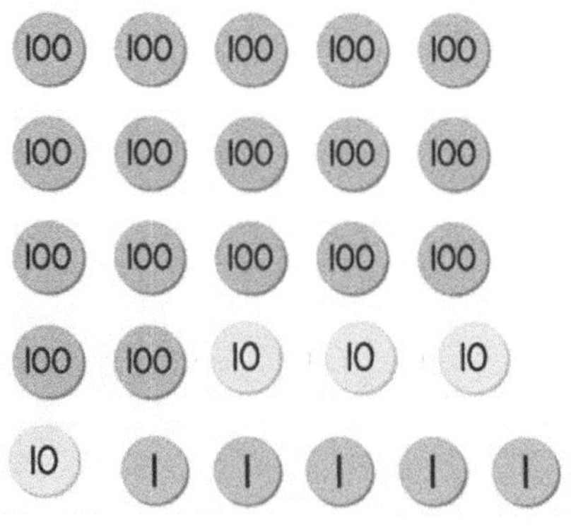

Figure 7.6 Student Activity

Concrete Student Activity

Guided Practice/ Checking for Understanding	The teacher passes out the problems. Students go around and share their work. **Carol:** I got the number 4,781. Way 1 was 4 thousands, 7 hundreds, 8 tens and 1 one. Way 2 was 3 thousands, 17 hundreds, 8 tens and 1 one. 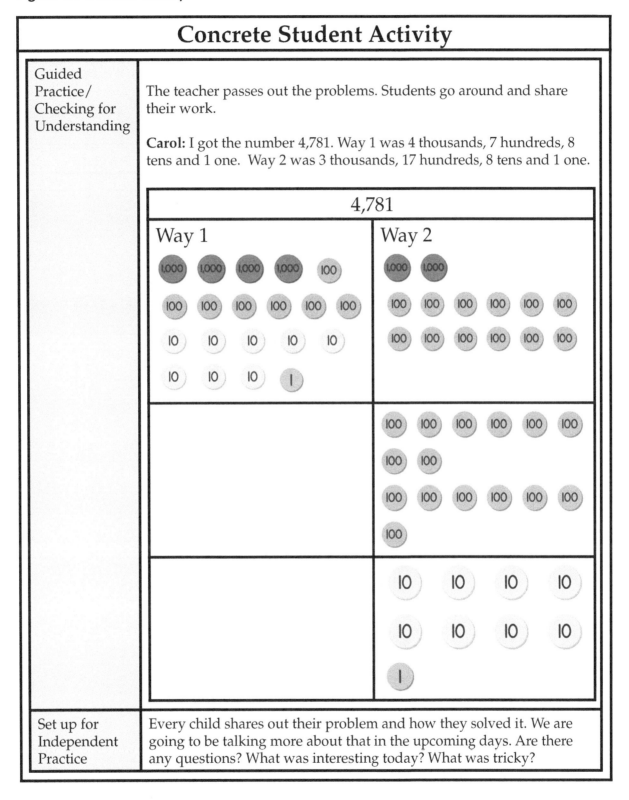
Set up for Independent Practice	Every child shares out their problem and how they solved it. We are going to be talking more about that in the upcoming days. Are there any questions? What was interesting today? What was tricky?

Figure 7.7 Lesson Close

Close
• What did we do today? • What was the math we were practicing? • What were we doing with our place value disks? • Was this easy or tricky? • Turn to a partner and state one thing you learned today.

Figure 7.8 Number Cards

1,233	2,389	326
4500	457	2703
2,222	789	3,008
4590	157	1,035

Visual Lesson

Figure 7.9 Visual Introduction

Introduction to Visual Explorations

Launch	**Teacher:** Today we are going to work on looking at how to represent numbers in a variety of ways. We will be working with place value disks and showing multiple representations. **Vocabulary:** thousands, hundreds, tens, ones, place value, expanded form, number name **Math Talk:** ____ and ___ make ____
Model	**Teacher:** I want to talk about how numbers can have multiple representations. Look at this card. What do you notice?

152

100 + 50 + 2	One hundred fifty-two
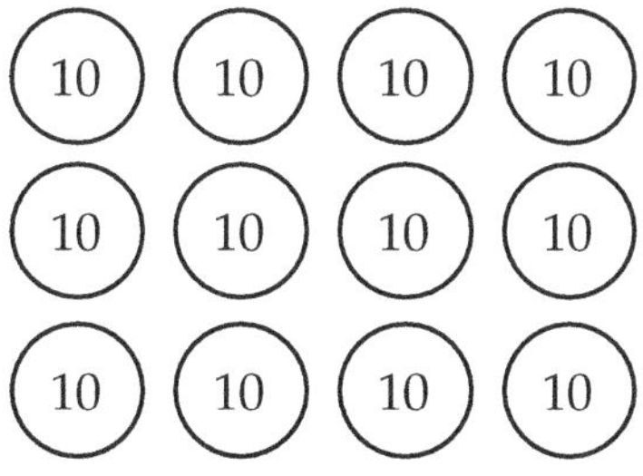 (10) (10) (10) (10) (10) (10) (10) (10) (10) (10) (10) (10)	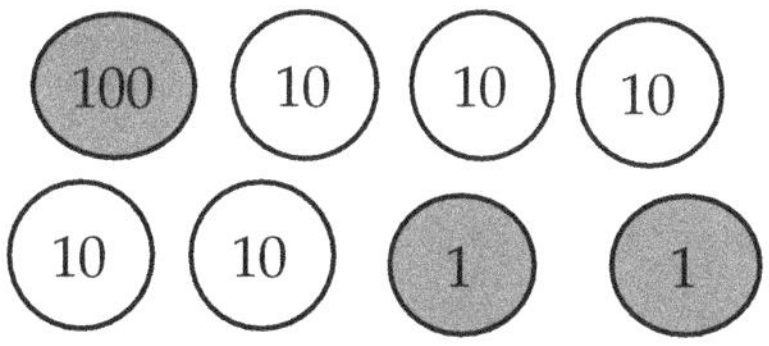 (100) (10) (10) (10) (10) (10) (1) (1)

(Continued)

Figure 7.9 (Continued)

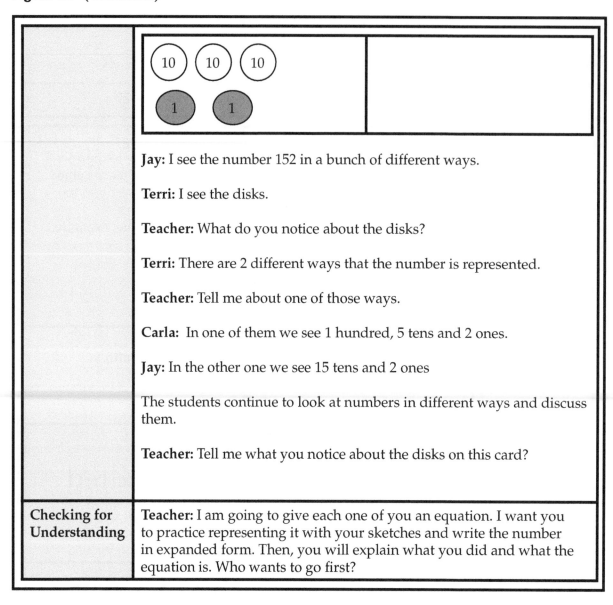

Jay: I see the number 152 in a bunch of different ways.

Terri: I see the disks.

Teacher: What do you notice about the disks?

Terri: There are 2 different ways that the number is represented.

Teacher: Tell me about one of those ways.

Carla: In one of them we see 1 hundred, 5 tens and 2 ones.

Jay: In the other one we see 15 tens and 2 ones

The students continue to look at numbers in different ways and discuss them.

Teacher: Tell me what you notice about the disks on this card?

Checking for Understanding	Teacher: I am going to give each one of you an equation. I want you to practice representing it with your sketches and write the number in expanded form. Then, you will explain what you did and what the equation is. Who wants to go first?

Figure 7.10 Student Activity

Visual Student Activity

Guided Practice/ Checking for Understanding	The teacher passes out cards with equations. Students pull a card and represent their thinking. The students each get a chance to share their problem and explain how they solved it. **Teacher:** Sketch out the answer. **Marta:** I sketched out 541 in 2 different ways. In the first one I did 5 hundreds, 4 ones and 1 one. In the second way I did 400 and 14 tens and 1 one. 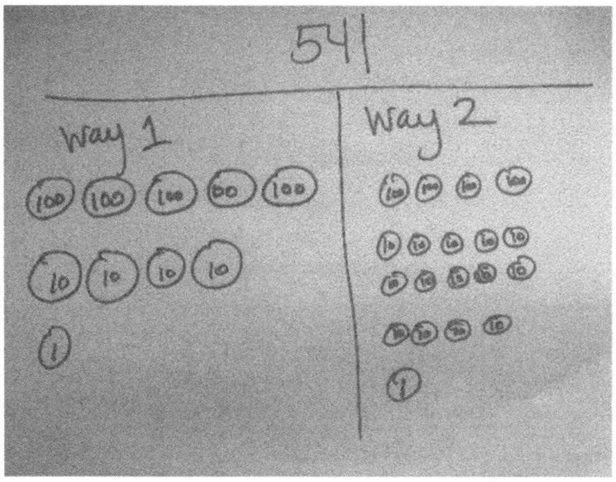 **Teacher:** Who agrees with Marta? Is she correct, if so explain why. **Dan:** I agree with Marta because you can see it in the drawing .
Set up for Independent Practice	*Teacher gives everybody a chance to do and discuss a problem. After everyone has shared the lesson ends.* We are going to be talking more about that in the upcoming days. Are there any questions? What was interesting today? What was tricky?

Figure 7.11 Lesson Close

Close
• What did we do today? • What was the math we were practicing? • What were we doing with our place value disks and sketches? • Was this easy or tricky? • Turn to a partner and state one thing you learned today.

Figure 7.12 Sketch Cards

289	475	202
188	575	102
379	398	232

Abstract Lesson

Figure 7.13 Abstract Introduction

Introduction to Abstract Explorations

Launch	**Teacher:** Today we are going to work on looking at how to represent numbers in a variety of ways. We will be working with place value disks.
	Vocabulary: thousands, hundreds, tens, ones, place value, expanded form, number name
	Math Talk: _____ and ___ make _____
	We are going to do a match. All the cards are mixed up and you will work with your partner to find 4 ways to name the number. Let's take a look at a set.
Model	$100 + 20 + 1$ One hundred twenty-one 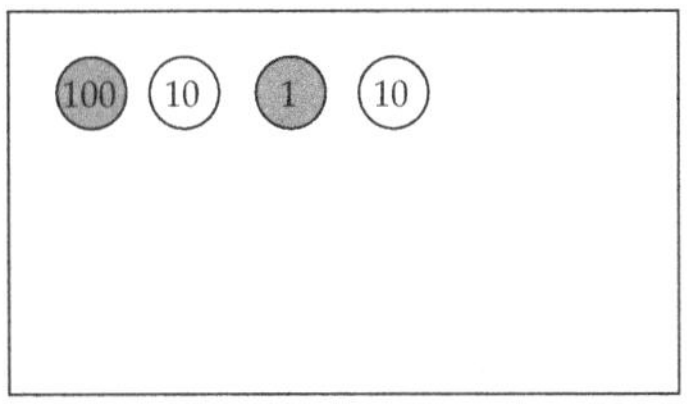 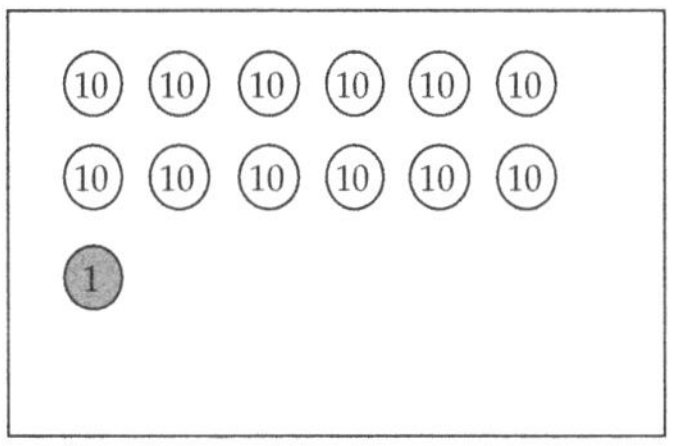 (100) (10) (1) (10) (10) (10) (10) (10) (10) (10) (10) (10) (10) (10) (10) (10) (1)
Checking for Understanding	**Teacher:** Ok, today that's what we are going to do. You each have a bag that you are going to share with your partner to work on finding all the sets.

Figure 7.14 Student Activity

Abstract Student Activity

Guided Practice/ Checking for Understanding	**Teacher:** Kelly and John, tell me about your story. **Kelly:** One card was 2 thousand 2 hundreds 2 tens and 2 ones. **John:** The other card was 2 thousands 12 hundreds and 2 ones. 2000 + 200 + 20 + 2 Two thousand two hundred and twenty-two 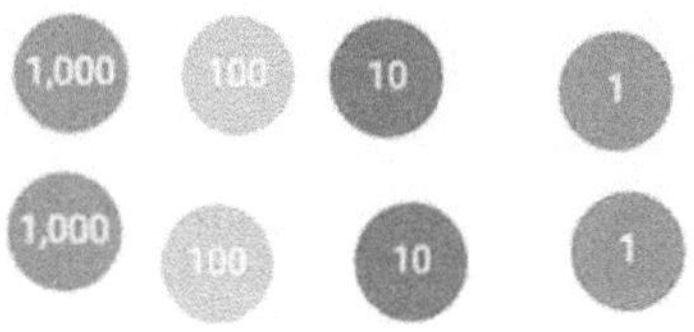 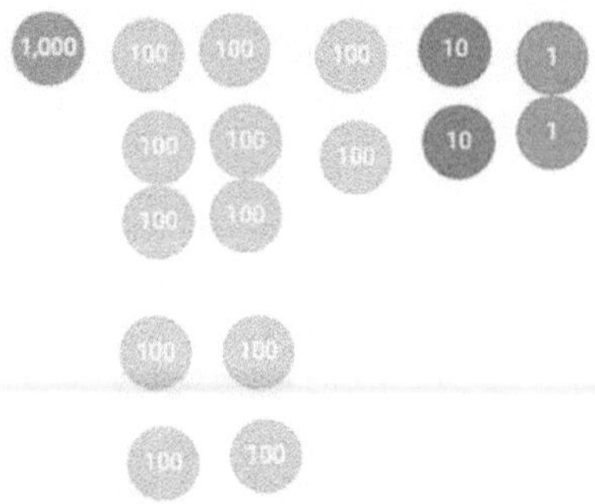
Set up for Independent Practice	The students take turns explaining their sets. **Teacher:** So what was the math we were studying today? **Tami:** We were looking at different ways to represent numbers. **Mark:** You can use expanded form. **Tracie:** You can use the number way. **Kim:** You can use place value disks but in different ways. **Teacher:** Ok, we are going to keep looking at how to name numbers in different ways. You may go to your workstations now.

Figure 7.15 Lesson Close

Close
• What did we do today? • What was the math we were practicing? • What were we doing with our sets of cards? • Was this easy or tricky? • Turn to a partner and state one thing you learned today.

Figure 7.16 Example of Card Sets

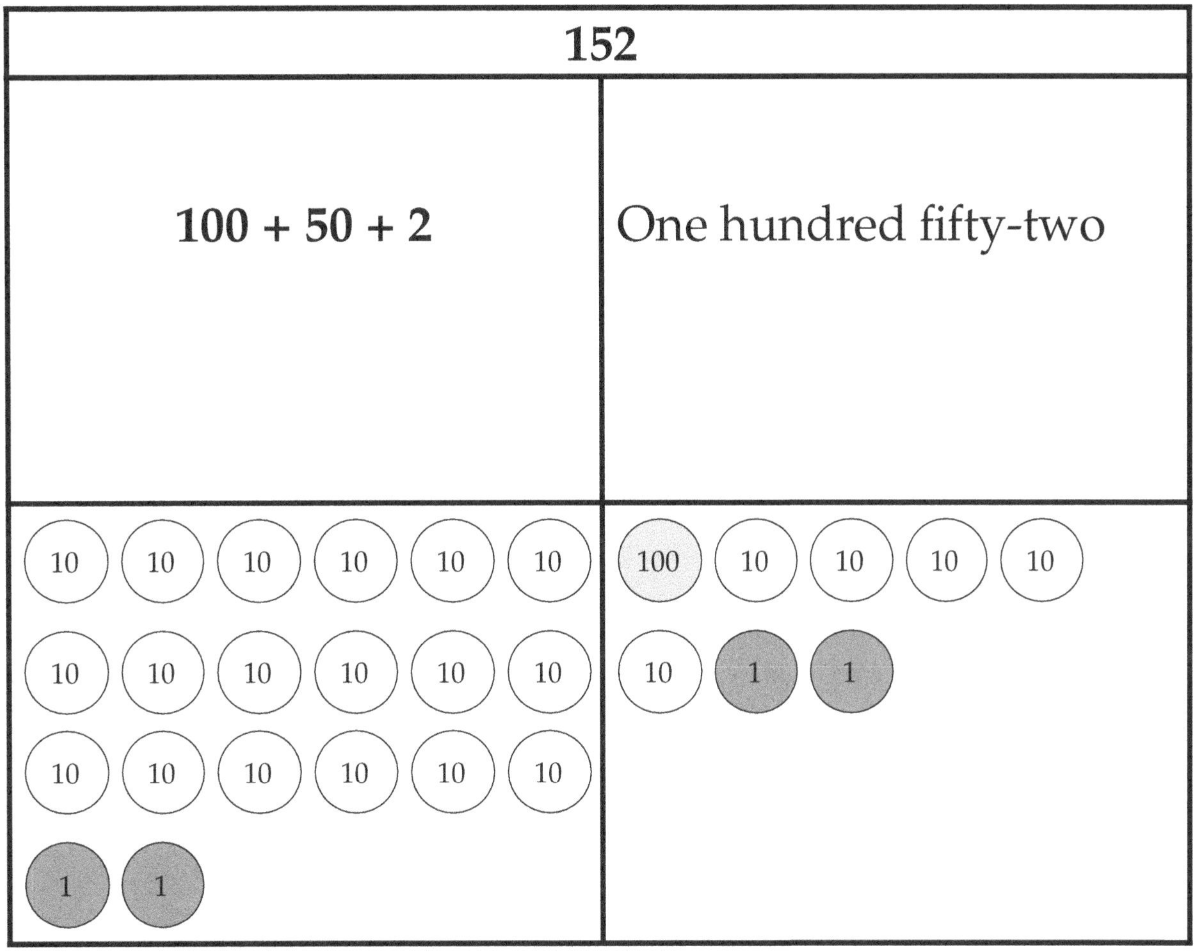

152	
100 + 50 + 2	One hundred fifty-two
10 10 10 10 10 10 10 10 10 10 10 10 10 10 10 10 10 10 1 1	100 10 10 10 10 10 1 1

Section Summary

When working on representing multi-digit numbers, it is important to have students build it, draw it and represent it with different models. You want to build flexibility around numbers. The point is to provide many opportunities for students to work with these ideas throughout the year, not only in the place value unit of study. The Number of the Day Routine is a great way to practice this throughout the year. In this routine students get to work on decomposing numbers, rounding numbers, operating on numbers, comparing numbers and more.

Rounding Numbers

Overview

Figure 7.17 Overview

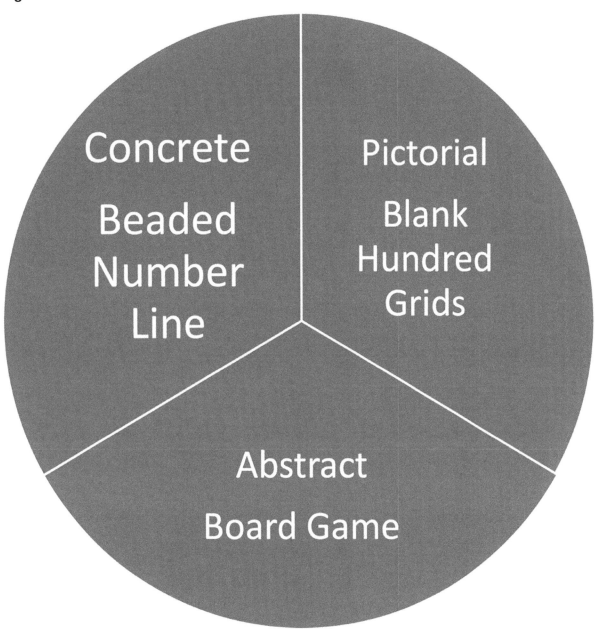

Figure 7.18 Planning Template

Introduction to Concrete Explorations: Rounding

Big Idea: Base Ten

Enduring Understanding: We can use various models to show rounding.

Essential Question: What are the ways to model rounding?

I can statement: I can round numbers to 1 million.

Materials
- Tools: Beaded Number lines
- Templates: 100's grid
- Cards
- Crayons

Cycle of Engagement

Concrete:

Pictorial: Drawing.

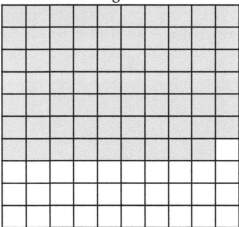

Abstract
67 rounds to 70

Vocabulary & Language Frames

- Count Up
- Count Back
- Compensate

Math Processes/Practices
- Problem Solving
- Reasoning
- Modeling
- Tools
- Structure
- Patterns

Figure 7.19 Differentiation

3 Differentiated Lessons
In this series of lessons, students are working on the concept of rounding numbers. They are developing this concept through concrete activities, pictorial activities and abstract activities. Here are some things to think about as you do these lessons.

Emerging	On Grade Level	Above Grade Level
Do a lot of work with rounding to 10 and 100 as a review.	The grade level standard is that students can round multi-digit numbers. Work through the cycle of concrete, pictorial and abstract representations.	Work with larger numbers.

 Looking for Misunderstandings and Common Errors

Students have get very confused when rounding. Spend time making sure they can round to the nearest 10 and 100 before going on to larger numbers. Use visual scaffolds for larger numbers.

Figure 7.20 Anchor Chart

Rounding

Concrete:

Pictorial: Drawing.

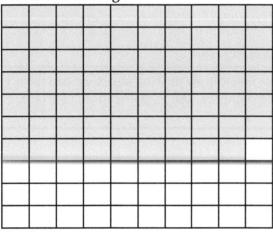

200 Grid

1	2	3	4	5	6	7	8	9	10
11	12	13	14	15	16	17	18	19	20
21	22	23	24	25	26	27	28	29	30
31	32	33	34	35	36	37	38	39	40
41	42	43	44	45	46	47	48	49	50
51	52	53	54	55	56	57	58	59	60
61	62	63	64	65	66	67	68	69	70
71	72	73	74	75	76	77	78	79	80
81	82	83	84	85	86	87	88	89	90
91	92	93	94	95	96	97	98	99	100
101	102	103	104	105	106	107	108	109	110
111	112	113	114	115	116	117	118	119	120
121	122	123	124	125	126	127	128	129	130
131	132	133	134	135	136	137	138	139	140
141	142	143	144	145	146	147	148	149	150
151	152	153	154	155	156	157	158	159	160
161	162	163	164	165	166	167	168	169	170
171	172	173	174	175	176	177	178	179	180
181	182	183	184	185	186	187	188	189	190
191	192	193	194	195	196	197	198	199	200

Abstract
67 rounds to 70

Concrete Lessons

Figure 7.21 Concrete Introduction

Introduction to Concrete Explorations

Launch	**Teacher:** Today we are going to work on rounding.
	
	Vocabulary: thousands, hundreds, tens, ones, place value, expanded form, number name
	
	Math Talk:
	    ____ rounds to ____
	    The nearest 10 is ____
	    The nearest 100 is ____

Model	**Teacher:** Today we are going to review and work on rounding with the beaded number line. I want you all to find 72 on your beaded number lines. What 2 tens does it sit between? What should it round to? 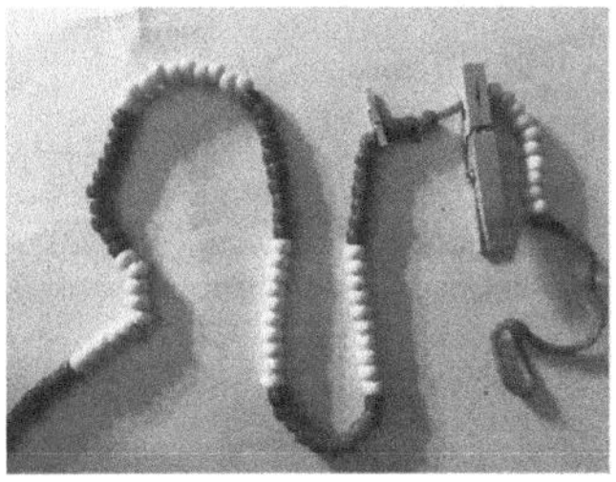 **Marcus:** 70 **Teacher:** Ok, now round 94 to the nearest ten. **Kimi:** It rounds to 90. The nearest hundred is 100.
Checking for Understanding	Teacher: Ok. I am going to give each one of you your own problem. I want you to read it. Solve it. Be ready to share how you did it. I am going to watch you and if you need help, look at our anchor charts, ask a partner and of course you can ask me.

Figure 7.22 Student Activity

Concrete Student Activity

Guided Practice/ Checking for Understanding	The teacher passes out the problems. Students pull a card and act out their problems. The students each get a chance to share their problem and explain how they solved it. **Teacher:** Ok, now round 48 to the nearest ten. 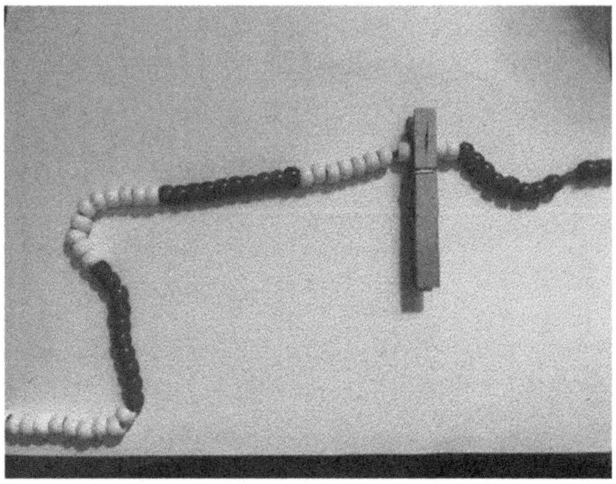 **Marcos.** It sits between 40 and 50. It rounds to 50.
Set up for Independent Practice	Every child shares out their problem and how they solved it. Teacher: We are going to be talking more about that in the upcoming days. Are there any questions? What was interesting today? What was tricky?

Figure 7.23 Lesson Close

Close

- What did we do today?
- What was the math we were practicing?
- What were we doing with our beaded number lines?
- Was this easy or tricky?
- Turn to a partner and state one thing you learned today.

Figure 7.24 Cards

34	29	49
55	61	78
88	91	11
Make up a problem.	Make up a problem.	Make up a problem.

Figure 7.25 Challenge version

Write a number that rounds to 10	Write a number that rounds to 20	Write a number that rounds to 30
Write a number that rounds to 40	Write a number that rounds to 50	Write a number that rounds to 60
Write a number that rounds to 70	Write a number that rounds to 80	Write a number that rounds to 90

Figure 7.25 Visual Introduction

Introduction to Visual explorations

Launch	Teacher: Today we are going to continue to work on rounding. We will be working with rounding grids.
	Vocabulary: thousands, hundreds, tens, ones, place value, expanded form, number name
	Math Talk: _____ rounds to _____ The nearest 10 is _____ The nearest 100 is _____
Model	Teacher: Today we are going to review rounding with visual templates. Use this template to round 554 to the nearest ten and the nearest 100. Sherry: It rounds to 550. The nearest 100 is 600.
Checking for Understanding	Teacher: I am going to give each one of you a problem. I want you to practice representing it with your hundred grid mats. Then, you will explain your thinking.

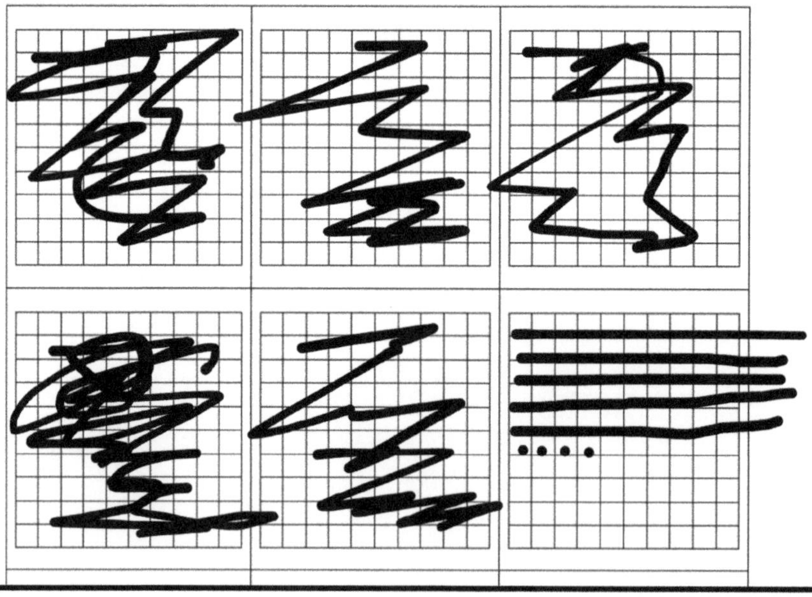

Figure 7.26 Student Activity

Visual Student Activity

Guided Practice/ Checking for Understanding	**Teacher:** Who wants to go? **Marcos:** I do. I had 787. It rounds to 780 (nearest 10). 800 is the nearest hundred. 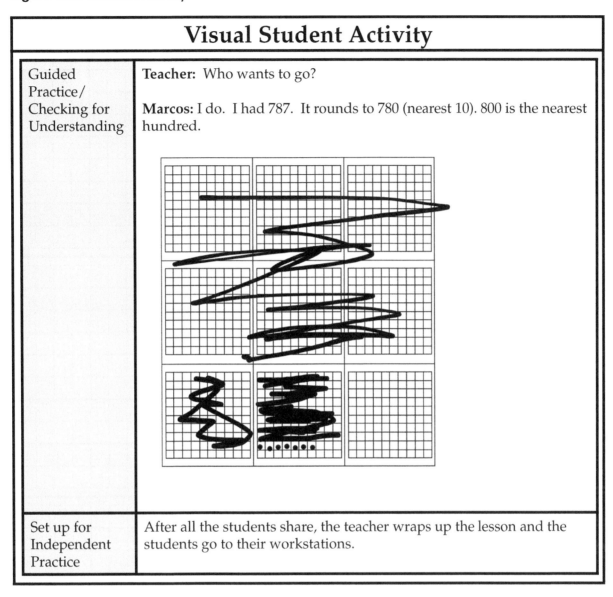
Set up for Independent Practice	After all the students share, the teacher wraps up the lesson and the students go to their workstations.

Figure 7.27 Lesson Close

Close

- What did we do today?
- What was the math we were practicing?
- What were we doing with our 100's grids?
- Was this easy or tricky?
- Turn to a partner and state one thing you learned today.

Figure 7.28 Hundred Grid Template

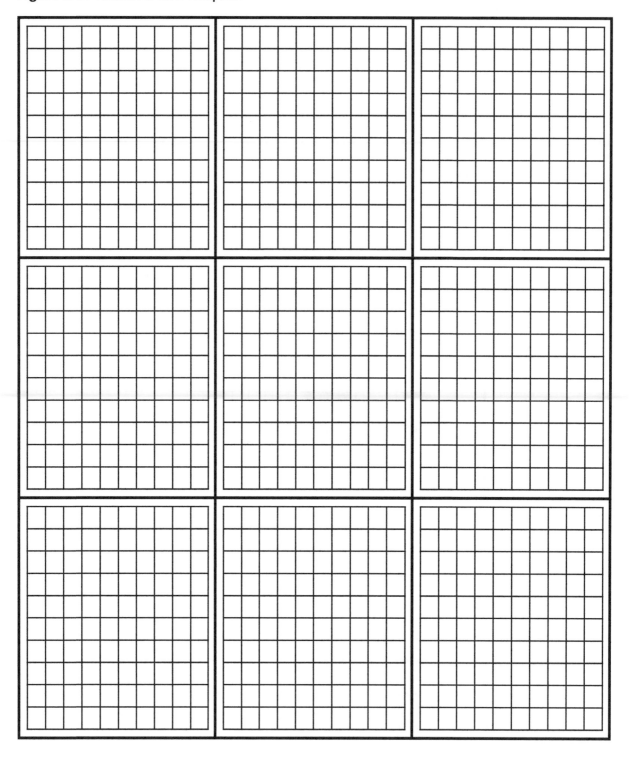

Abstract Lessons

Figure 7.29 Abstract Introduction

Introduction to Abstract Explorations

Launch	**Teacher:** Today we are going to work on rounding with a game.
	Vocabulary: thousands, hundreds, tens, ones, place value, expanded form, number name
	Math Talk: ____ rounds to ____ The nearest 10 is ____ The nearest 100 is ____
Model	**Teacher:** We are going to play a board game where you land on a number and have to round it. If you are correct, you stay there. If you are incorrect you move back 1 space. Whoever reaches finish first wins the game. 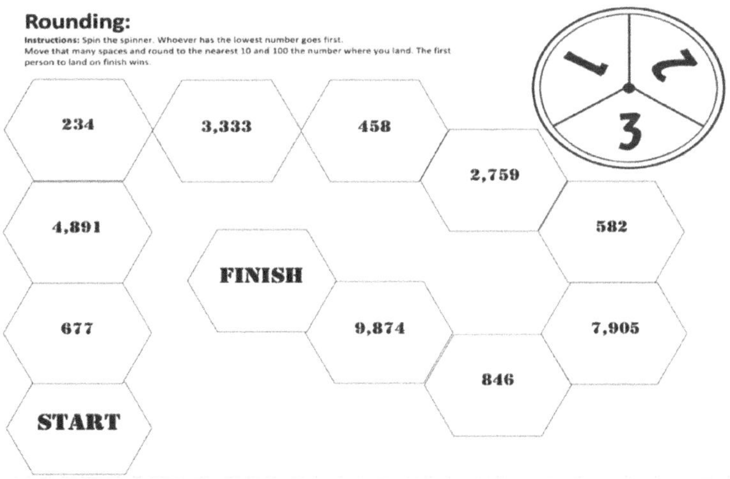 **Rounding:** **Instructions:** Spin the spinner. Whoever has the lowest number goes first. Move that many spaces and round to the nearest 10 and 100 the number where you land. The first person to land on finish wins. 234 3,333 458 2,759 582 4,891 FINISH 7,905 677 9,874 846 START
Checking for Understanding	**Teacher:** You are going to play with a partner or in a group of 3. Any questions?

Figure 7.30 Student Activity

Abstract Student Activity	
Guided Practice/ Checking for Understanding	Teacher watches, takes notes and asks questions. **Teacher:** Kayla, tell me how you solved that problem. **Kayla:** I landed on 7,905. The nearest ten is 7,910 and the nearest hundred is 7900.
Set up for Independent Practice	**Teacher:** We are going to be talking more about this in the upcoming days. Are there any questions? What was interesting today? What was tricky?

Figure 7.31 Lesson Close

Close
• What did we do today? • What was the math we were practicing? • What were we doing on our board game? • Was this easy or tricky? • Turn to a partner and state one thing you learned today.

Figure 7.32 Rounding Game

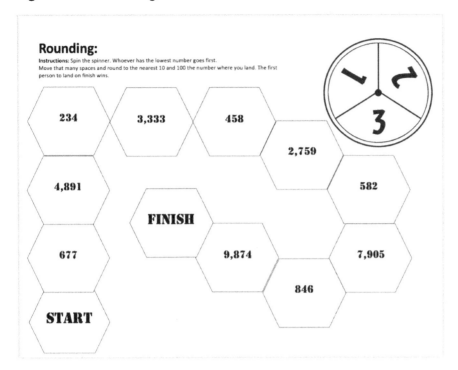

Figure 7.33 Challenge Version

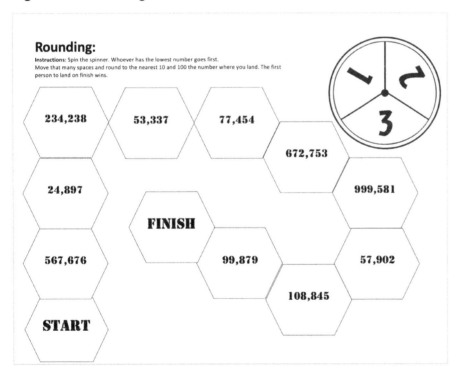

Section Summary

Rounding is an important skill that is deeply connected to estimating. Students need to estimate when they are problem solving. Many times, we rush through this skill with songs and poems and students don't really conceptually understand what they are doing. It is always good to review the third grade standards of rounding to ten and the nearest hundred first and then go on to larger numbers. Teachers should build the concept through using beaded number lines, marked number lines and open number lines. Also, blank hundred grids provide a great visual for students to visualize what they are doing when they are rounding. Before we jump to abstract games, we must make sure that students can explain what they are doing and how they are doing it.

Multiplying a 1-Digit Number by a 2-Digit Number

Overview

Figure 7.34 Overview

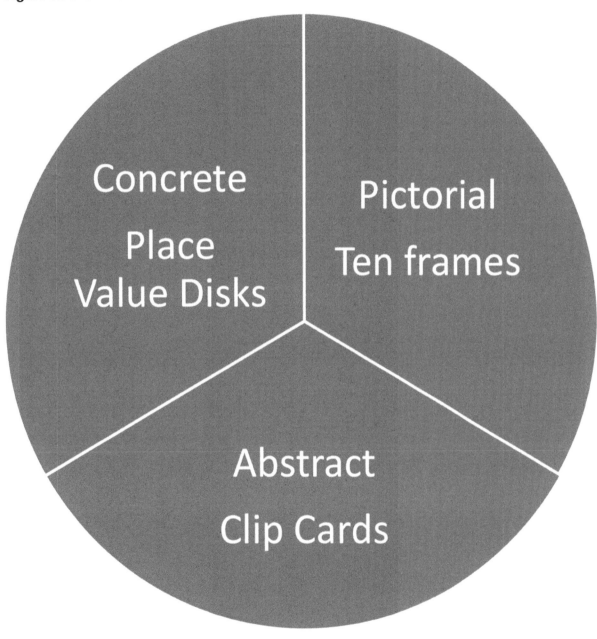

Figure 7.35 Planning Template

Multiplying Multi-digit Numbers

Big Idea: Base Ten; Operation Meanings & Relationships

Enduring Understanding: We can model problems in many ways.

Essential Question: What are the ways to model multi-digit multiplication?

I can statement: I can multiply multi-digit numbers

Materials
- Tools: Place Value Disks
- Multiplication templates based on multiplier
- Cards
- Ten Frames

Cycle of Engagement

Concrete:

Concrete 3 × 43

10 10 10 10 ① ① ①	10 10 10 10 ① ① ①	10 10 10 10 ① ① ①
43	43	43
3 × 43 = 129		

Abstract: 34 × 5

5 × 30 = 150

5 × 4 = 20

150 + 20 = 170

Vocabulary & Language Frames

Vocabulary: thousands, hundreds, tens, ones, place value, multiply, product, factors

Math talk: My strategy was to _____.

Pictorial: Drawing
5 × 25 = 125

ll	ll	ll	ll	ll
••• ••	•• • ••	••••••	••••• •	••••• •
25	25	25	25	25

Figure 7.36 Differentiation

3 Differentiated Lessons		
In this series of lessons, students are working on the concept of multiplying multi-digit numbers. They are developing this concept through concrete activities, pictorial activities and abstract activities. Here are some things to think about as you do these lessons.		
Emerging	**On Grade Level**	**Above Grade Level**
Do a lot of work with strategies. Use the place value disks and base ten blocks.	The standard is that students understand a variety of strategies.	Extend number range.
Looking for Misunderstandings and Common Errors		
Multiplying multi-digit numbers is tricky for students, partly because many of them are still struggling with single-digit multiplication. When teaching multi-digit multiplication the emphasis should be on different strategies not the traditional algorithm. Students should be thinking about different ways to put together and break apart numbers in order to multiply them and then be able to explain their thinking.		

Figure 7.37 Anchor Chart

Concrete

3×52

10 10	10 10	10 10
10 10	10 10	10 10
10	10	10
① ①	① ①	① ①
52	52	52
$3 \times 52 = 150 + 6 = 156$		

Pictorial

$3 \times 29 = 60 + 27 = 87$

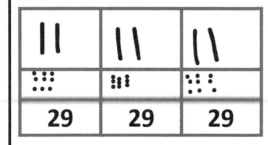

29	29	29

Abstract

$17 \times 8 =$

$8 \times 10 = 80$

$8 \times 7 = 56$

$80 + 56 = 136$

Concrete Lesson

Figure 7.38 Concrete Introduction

	Introduction to Concrete Explorations
Launch	**Teacher:** Today we are going to work on looking at how to multiply 2-digit numbers with place value disks. **Vocabulary:** thousands, hundreds, tens, ones, place value, multiply, product, factors **Math Talk:** ____ and ___ make ____
Model	**Teacher:** Today we are going to practice multiplying a one-digit number by a two- digit number with place value disks. Here are your multiplying mats. So, if we are multiplying by 3 then we have 3 columns and if we are multiplying by 4, then we have 4 columns. We are doing this right now so we can look at this idea of multiplication as repeated addition. As well as we can see how to break apart numbers and add them back up by their place values. This is easy to see with the place value disks. Let's take a look. Our first problem is 3×41. Everybody set it up. Ok, who wants to explain. **Kimi: I see 120 + 3 and that makes 123.** **Teacher:** Yes, so we can break that apart and first multiply the tens and then the ones and then put them back together.

10 10 10 10 ①	10 10 10 10 ①	10 10 10 10 ①
41	41	41
$3 \times 41 = 120 + 3 = 123$		

Teacher: Let's do another one. Who wants to explain?

Raul: I see 200 plus 12 so that makes 212.

Figure 7.38 (Continued)

	Teacher: So, you first multiplied the tens and then the ones. And we can say to do that but you all can actually see it with the place value disks. 4×53 | 10 10	10 10	10 10	10 10
10 10	10 10	10 10	10 10
10 (1)	10 (1)	10 (1)	10 (1)
(1) (1)	(1) (1)	(1) (1)	(1) (1)
53	53	53	53	 $4 \times 53 = 200 + 12 = 212$
Checking for Understanding	*Teacher reads 2 more problems that the group discusses.* **Teacher:** Ok. I am going to give each one of you your own problem. I want you to read it. Solve it. Be ready to share how you did it. I am going to watch you and if you need help, look at our anchor charts, ask a partner and of course you can ask me.

Figure 7.39 Student Activity

Concrete Student Activities

Guided Practice/ Checking for Understanding	**Teacher:** Our next problem is 4 × 25. Who wants to go? **Tami:** I will. But I know the answer already because it's 4 quarters which is a dollar or 100. I modeled it too. I did 80 + 20 = 100. <table><tr><td>10 10 ① ① ① ① ①</td><td>10 10 ① ① ① ① ①</td><td>10 10 ① ① ① ① ①</td><td>10 10 ① ① ① ① ①</td></tr><tr><td>25</td><td>25</td><td>25</td><td>25</td></tr><tr><td colspan="4" align="center">4 × 25 = 80 + 20 = 100</td></tr></table>
Set up for Independent Practice	Every child shares out their problem and how they solved it with the place value disks. **Teacher:** We are going to be talking more about this in the upcoming days. Are there any questions? What was interesting today? What was tricky?

Figure 7.40 Lesson Close

Close

- What did we do today?
- What was the math we were practicing?
- What were we doing with our place value disks?
- Was this easy or tricky?
- Turn to a partner and state one thing you learned today.

Figure 7.41 Place Value Disks

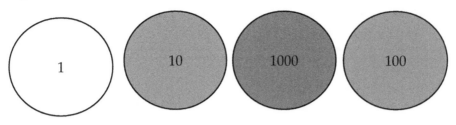

Figure 7.42 Multiplying Mats

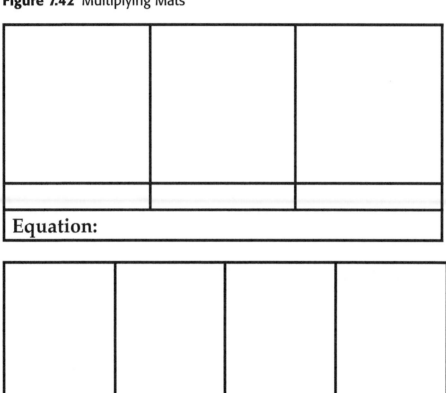

Visual Lesson

Figure 7.43 Visual Introduction

Introduction to Visual Explorations

Launch	**Teacher:** Today we are going to work on looking at how to multiply 2-digit numbers with math sketches. **Vocabulary:** thousands, hundreds, tens, ones, place value, multiply, product, factors **Math Talk:** ____ and ___ make ____
Model	**Teacher:** Today we are going to practice multiplying a one-digit number by a two-digit number with math sketches. So first we are going to sketch 5×37. Everybody do it. Ok, who wants to explain their sketch? **Yesenia:** I do. I did 5 groups of 30 and then 5 groups of 7. When I put it together I get 150 plus 35 and that makes 185. Does everybody see that? 5×37 **Teacher:** So you are breaking it apart and multiplying the tens first and then the ones and then putting it all back together.
Checking for Understanding	**Teacher:** Who wants to go next?

(Continued)

Figure 7.43 (Continued)

Hong: I do. I multiplied 3 × 30 and then 3 × 9 and that makes 90 + 27 which is 117.

3 × 39

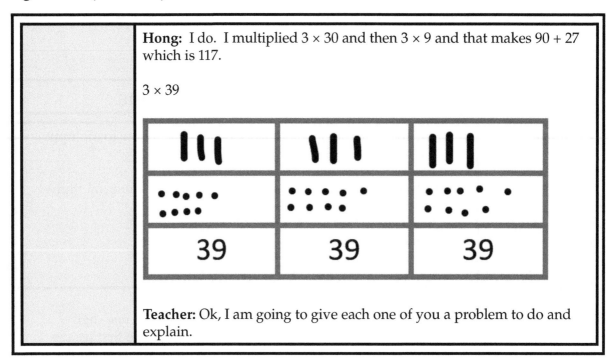

Teacher: Ok, I am going to give each one of you a problem to do and explain.

Figure 7.44 Student Activity

Visual Student Activity

Guided Practice/ Checking for Understanding	The teacher passes out cards with equations. Students pull a card and solve it. The students each get a chance to share their problem and explain how they **Teacher:** Who wants to go next? **Tracie:** I do. I multiplied 3×10 and then 3×9 and that makes $30 + 27$ which is 57. 3×19 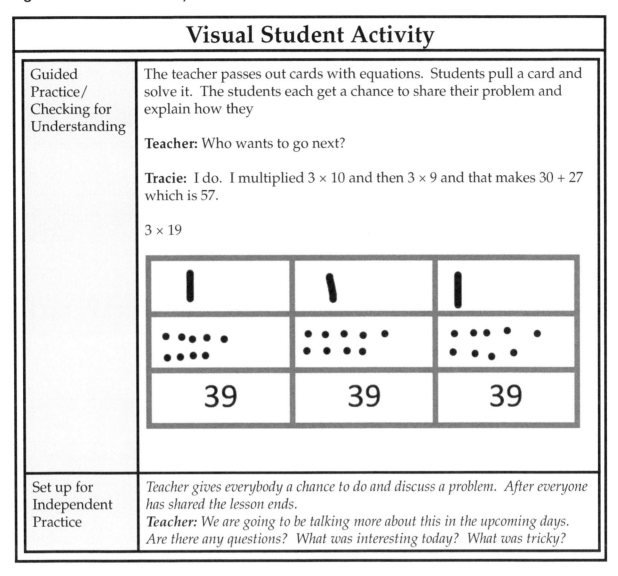
Set up for Independent Practice	*Teacher gives everybody a chance to do and discuss a problem. After everyone has shared the lesson ends.* ***Teacher:*** *We are going to be talking more about this in the upcoming days. Are there any questions? What was interesting today? What was tricky?*

Figure 7.45 Lesson Close

Close

- What did we do today?
- What was the math we were practicing?
- What were we doing with our math sketches?
- Was this easy or tricky?
- Turn to a partner and state one thing you learned today.

Figure 7.46 Drawing Mats

tens	tens	tens	tens	tens
ones	ones	ones	ones	ones

tens	tens	tens	tens	tens	tens
ones	ones	ones	ones	ones	ones

Figure 7.47 Expression Cards

5×25	3×44
6×37	7×28
4×55	9×16
3×28	2×63
3×15	Make up your own problem!

The 7 and 9 questions may be too big for the mats shown.

Figure 7.48 Abstract Introduction

Introduction to Abstract Explorations

Launch	**Teacher:** Today we are going to work multiplying 2-digit numbers. **Vocabulary:** thousands, hundreds, tens, ones, place value, multiply, product, factors **Math Talk:** _____ and ___ make _____
Model	**Teacher:** Today we are going to practice multiplying a one-digit number by a two-digit number through a game of war. You are going to each pull a card and whoever has the largest product wins the cards. When all the cards are gone, whoever has the most pairs wins. <table><tr><td>4×50</td><td>3×39</td><td>7×18</td></tr><tr><td>8×19</td><td>2×75</td><td>4×22</td></tr><tr><td>9×25</td><td>5×61</td><td>6×70</td></tr><tr><td>4×33</td><td>5×25</td><td>8×25</td></tr></table> **Teacher:** Let's play a round. **Maite:** I pulled 4×50 and that is 200. I know this because $50 + 50 + 50 + 50$ is 200. **Joe:** I pulled 3×39. I know that 3×30 is 90 plus 27 and that makes 117. Maite wins the pair of cards.
Checking for Understanding	**Teacher:** So who can explain how we play? **Marvin:** It's like war but we are doing multi-digit numbers. You pull and your partner pulls and you say your products. Whoever has the largest product wins! Let's go!

Figure 7.49 Student Activity

	Abstract Student Activity
Guided Practice/ Checking for Understanding	**Teacher:** Lucy and Hong tell me what you did this round. **Lucy:** I pulled 2 × 75 and that is 150. I know this because 75 plus 75 is 150. **Hong:** I pulled 4 × 22 and that make 88. I know this because 4 × 20 is 80 and 8 more make 88. So Lucy wins this pair.
Set up for Independent Practice	The students continue to play the game until they are done. The teacher watches how the students are doing, who knows the answer right away and who gets stuck. She also notices who has to use their tools and who just knows it by heart.

Figure 7.50 Lesson Close

Close
• What did we do today? • What was the math we were practicing? • What were we doing with our game of war? • Was this easy or tricky? • Turn to a partner and state one thing you learned today.

Figure 7.51 Number Cards

2×32	4×44	7×56
9×88	3×90	5×28
6×61	9×99	7×29
4×29	8×32	9×17
7×77	2×64	5×55

Section Summary

Multiplying multi-digit numbers can be tricky. The lessons in this section show how to build conceptual understanding. Working with the place value disks, students can actually see the place and value of the numbers and then think and talk about how to take them apart and put them back together as a strategy to multiply. Having students do sketches also reinforces this idea of working flexibly with numbers. Way before you have students learn and work with the traditional algorithm, they should have many different ways to think about multiplying. There are many other strategies such as doubling and halving and using partial products (what we were doing here). There are also models like the open array. Students need to be really comfortable when they see multi-digit numbers. They need to feel like they have many different ways to approach a problem.

Dividing a Double-Digit Number by a Single-Digit Number

Overview

Figure 7.52 Overview

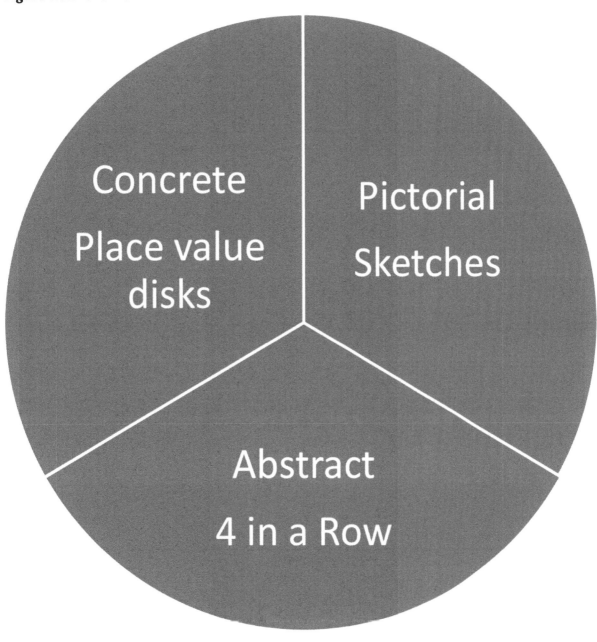

Figure 7.53 Dividing a Double-Digit Number by a Single-Digit Number

Dividing a Double-Digit Number by a Single-Digit Number	
Big Idea: Place Value; Operation Meanings & Algorithms **Enduring Understanding:** Students will understand that there are different strategies to divide. **Essential Question:** What are the ways to model dividing numbers? **I can statement:** I can divide numbers using different strategies and models.	**Materials** • Tools: Place Value Disks • Division Templates • Cards
Cycle of Engagement **Concrete:** $38 \div 3$ There is a remainder of 2 **Pictorial: Drawing** $38 \div 3 = 12$ • • There is a remainder of 2.	Vocabulary & Language Frames • Tens, Ones, Hundreds • Division • Dividing • Divisor • Dividend • Quotient • Open Array • Partial quotients **My partial quotients are** _____. **Abstract:** $38 \div 3 = 12r2$ There is a remainder of 2.

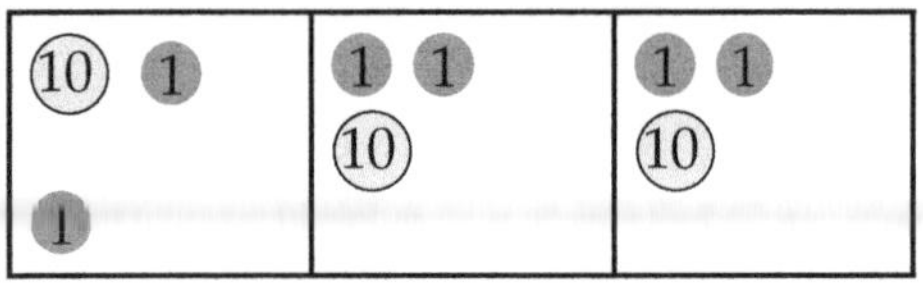

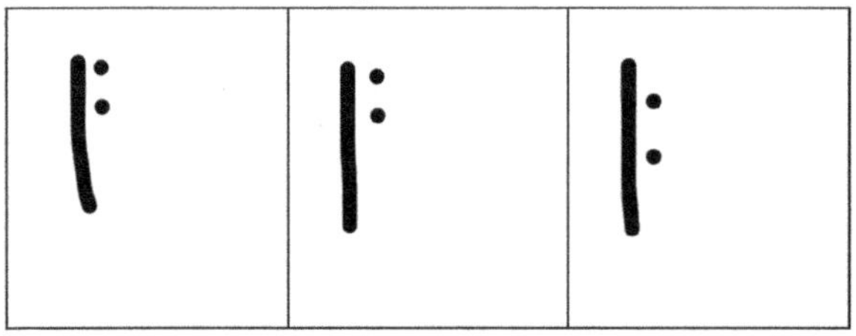

Figure 7.54 Differentiation

3 Differentiated Lessons
In this series of lessons, students are working on the concept of dividing a 2-digit number by a 1-digit number. They are developing this concept through concrete activities, pictorial activities and abstract activities. Here are some things to think about as you do these lessons.

Emerging	On Grade Level	Above Grade Level
Do a lot of work with students using base ten blocks and place value disks.	Make sure students can sketch their thinking.	Work with larger numbers.

 Looking for Misunderstandings and Common Errors

The focus here should be that students understand the concept of division.

Figure 7.55 Anchor Chart

Base Ten Blocks

Concrete:
38 ÷ 3

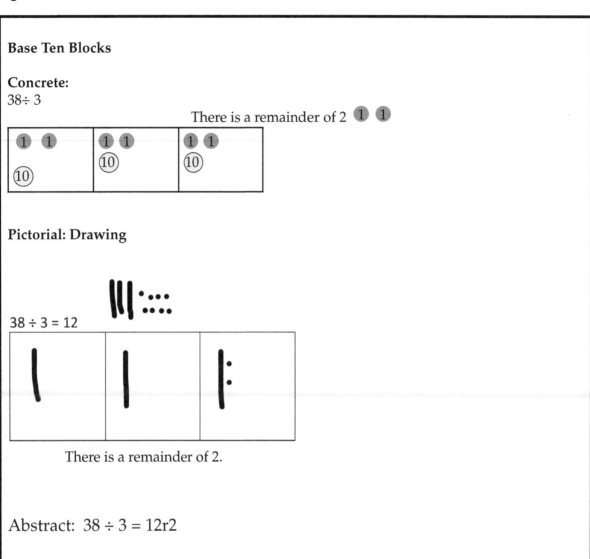

There is a remainder of 2

Pictorial: Drawing

38 ÷ 3 = 12

There is a remainder of 2.

Abstract: 38 ÷ 3 = 12r2

Concrete Lessons

Figure 7.56 Concrete Introduction

Introduction to Concrete Explorations

Launch	**Teacher:** Today we are going to work on how to divide 2-digit numbers with place value disks. **Vocabulary:** thousands, hundreds, tens, ones, place value, multiply, product, dividend, divisors, quotient, partial quotients **Math Talk:** My partial quotients are _____.
Model	**Teacher:** How could we solve this problem with our place value disks? Everybody do it and then somebody explain your thinking. **Missy:** I divided it into 3 parts. I got 14 and there is a remainder of 2. Did everybody else get that? (students indicate that they did). $44 \div 3$

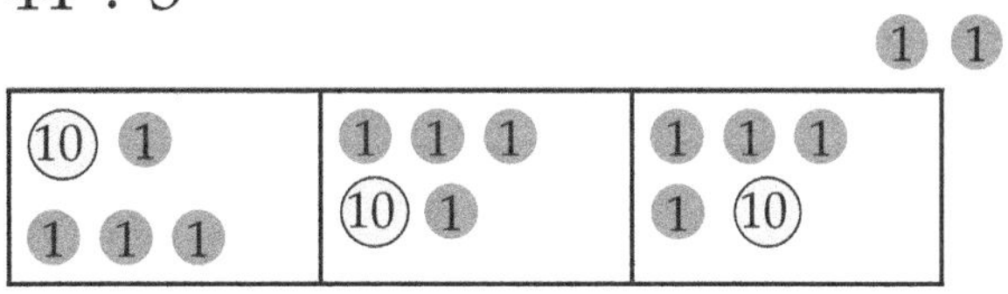

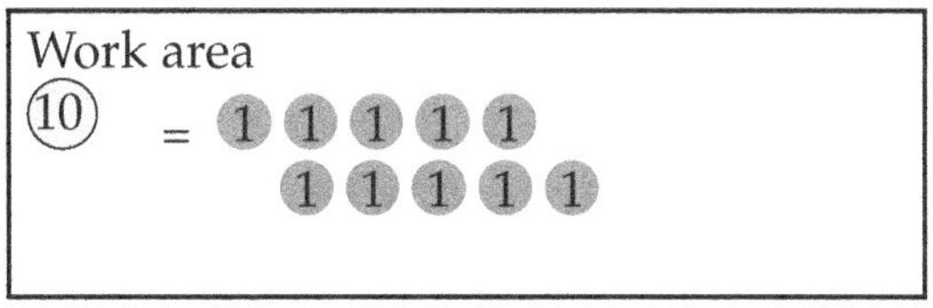

(Continued)

Figure 7.56 (Continued)

Checking for Understanding	Teacher: Who wants to do another one?
	David: I divided it into 3 parts. I got 10 and there is a remainder of 1. Did everybody else get that? (students indicate that they did). 31 ÷ 3 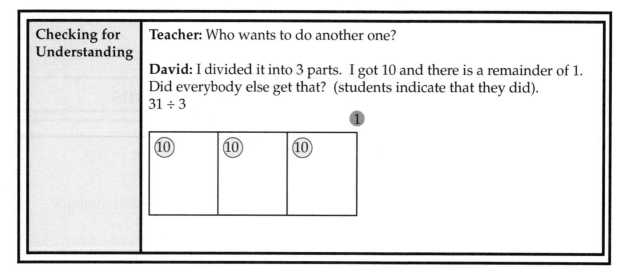

Figure 7.57 Student Activity

	Concrete Student Activity
Guided Practice/ Checking for Understanding	**Teacher:** Ok, who wants to go next **Grace:** I got 3. That was easy. 3 people each get 10. $30 \div 3 = 3$ 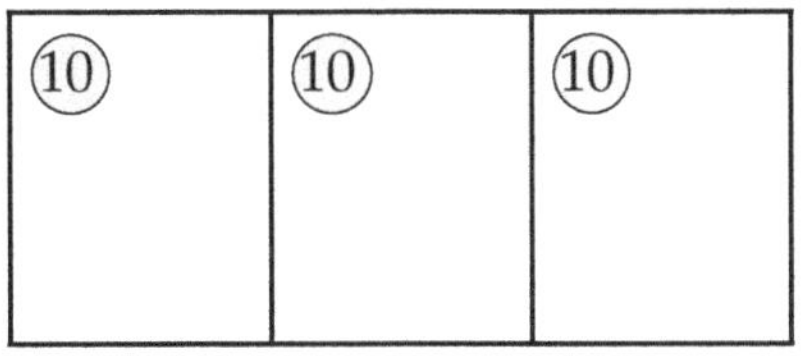 ⑩ ⑩ ⑩
Set up for Independent Practice	Every child shares out their problem and how they solved it. We are going to be talking more about that in the upcoming days. Are there any questions? What was interesting today? What was tricky?

Figure 7.58 Lesson Close

Close
• What did we do today? • What was the math we were practicing? • What were we doing with our place value disks? • Was this easy or tricky? • Turn to a partner and state one thing you learned today.

Figure 7.59 Cards

$31 \div 3$	$93 \div 6$
$52 \div 9$	$71 \div 2$
$68 \div 7$	$89 \div 8$
$29 \div 4$	$44 \div 5$
$27 \div 6$	$38 \div 7$
$42 \div 8$	$55 \div 9$
$65 \div 7$	$75 \div 9$

Visual Lessons

Figure 7.60 Visual Introduction

Introduction to a Visual Activity

Launch	**Teacher:** Today we are going to work on looking at how to divide 2-digit numbers with place value disks. **Vocabulary:** thousands, hundreds, tens, ones, place value, multiply, product, dividend, divisors, quotient, partial quotients **Math Talk:** My partial quotients are _____.
Model	**Teacher:** Today I am going to give you a problem. I want you solve it with a math sketch. (Students work on the problem) Ok, who wants to share their thinking. **Marvin:** I did this. I had 38 and I know 30 divided by 10 is 3 and then 8 divided by 3 is 2 with a remainder of 2 … so put those together and you get 12 with a remainder of 2. $38 \div 3$
Checking for Understanding	**Teacher:** Who wants to go next? **Harold:** I''ll go. I had 61. So I know that 50 divided by 5 is 10 and 55 is 11 and 60 is 12… so there is 1 leftover.

(Continued)

Figure 7.60 (Continued)

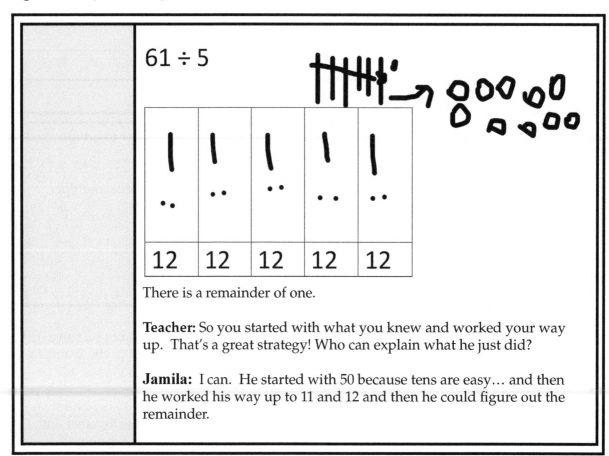

$61 \div 5$

There is a remainder of one.

Teacher: So you started with what you knew and worked your way up. That's a great strategy! Who can explain what he just did?

Jamila: I can. He started with 50 because tens are easy… and then he worked his way up to 11 and 12 and then he could figure out the remainder.

Figure 7.61 Visual Student Activity

Visual Student Activity

Guided Practice/ Checking for Understanding	**Teacher:** Who wants to go next? **Sue:** I"ll go. I know that 4×6 is 24… and that there is 3 left over… I modeled it like this…. $27 \div 4$ 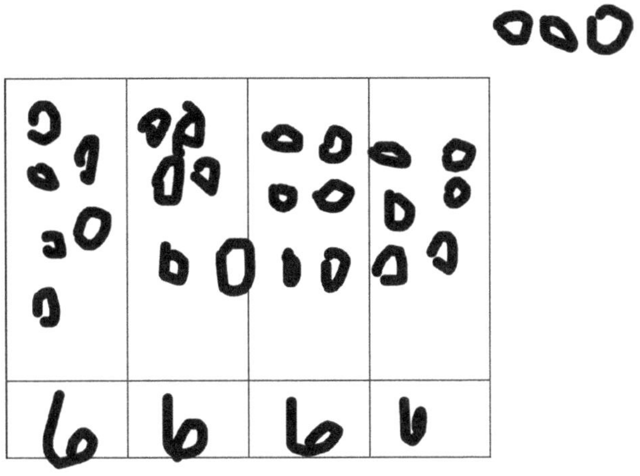
Set up for Independent Practice	*Teacher gives everybody a chance to do and discuss a problem. After everyone has shared the lesson ends.* We are going to be talking more about this in the upcoming days. Are there any questions? What was interesting today? What was tricky?

Figure 7.62 Lesson Close

Close

- What did we do today?
- What was the math we were practicing?
- What were we doing with our math sketches?
- Was this easy or tricky?
- Turn to a partner and state one thing you learned today.

Figure 7.63 Cards

$41 \div 3$	$83 \div 6$
$52 \div 9$	$91 \div 2$
$38 \div 7$	$79 \div 8$
$62 \div 4$	$27 \div 5$
$17 \div 6$	$48 \div 7$
$26 \div 8$	$37 \div 9$
$58 \div 7$	$92 \div 9$

Abstract Lessons

Figure 7.64 Abstract Introduction

Introduction to Abstract Explorations

Launch	**Teacher:** Today we are going to work on looking at how to divide 2-digit numbers with a game. **Vocabulary:** thousands, hundreds, tens, ones, place value, multiply, product, dividend, divisors, quotient, partial quotients **Math Talk:** The partial quotients are _____.
Model	**Teacher:** Today we are going to practice dividing a 2-digit number by a one -digit number through a game of war. You are going to each pull a card and whoever has the largest quotient wins the cards. When all the cards are gone, whoever has the most pairs wins. Let's do a sample round. $52 \div 4$ $32 \div 3$ **Maite:** I pulled 52 divided by 4. I know 40 divided by 4 is 10 and 12 divided by 4 is 3. That is 13. I have the bigger quotient. I win the pair. **Joey:** I pulled $32 \div 3$. That is $30 \div 3$ which is 10 and then a remainder of 2. So my quotient is smaller than Maite's.
Checking for Understanding	**Teacher:** Ok... let's do another one... **Lucas:** I pulled 67 divided by 8...if I think multiplication. 8×8 is 64 and so it is 8 with 3 left over. **Tom:** I pulled 88 divided by 3... so I broke it up... I know 60 divided by 3 is 20 ... and then 28 divided by 3 is 9 with 1 left over... so it's 29 with 1 left over... I win the pair.

Figure 7.65 Student Activity

<table>
<tr><td colspan="2" align="center">**Abstract Student Activity**</td></tr>
<tr>
<td>Guided Practice/ Checking for Understanding</td>
<td>Students play the game with a partner and the teacher listens, takes notes and asks questions. He is noticing who is doing it with paper and pencil, who is using the manipulatives and who is using a strategy. Also, the teacher is listening to see who can explain their thinking.

Teacher: Marvin and Kayla tell me about your round.

Marvin: I pulled $48 \div 5$... that's almost 10 because 50 divided by 5 is 10 so it must be 9 and some leftovers. Wait, I know 9×5 is 45 so, 3 left over...

Kayla: I pulled $55 \div 5$ and that is 11 because 5×11 is 55. I win both cards.</td>
</tr>
<tr>
<td>Set up for Independent Practice</td>
<td>The teacher continues to ask the students questions about their strategies as they play the game. The teacher is taking notes as the students play. They are using their different strategies to explain their thinking.</td>
</tr>
</table>

Figure 7.66 Lesson Close

<table>
<tr><td align="center">**Close**</td></tr>
<tr><td>

- What did we do today?
- What was the math we were practicing?
- What were we doing with our game of war cards?
- Was this easy or tricky?
- Are there any questions?

</td></tr>
</table>

Figure 7.67 Easy Version of Cards and Hard Version of Cards

$31 \div 3$	$25 \div 6$	$43 \div 4$
$27 \div 5$	$25 \div 2$	$29 \div 7$
$65 \div 8$	$91 \div 9$	$17 \div 2$
$19 \div 3$	$17 \div 4$	$33 \div 5$

$38 \div 3$	$41 \div 5$	$55 \div 6$
$79 \div 5$	$24 \div 2$	$64 \div 7$
$88 \div 3$	$91 \div 5$	$50 \div 6$
$99 \div 5$	$29 \div 3$	$33 \div 7$

Section Summary

When working with the fourth graders on dividing double-digit numbers by single-digit numbers it is important to take them through the cycle of concrete, pictorial and abstract. They have to see it and work with different manipulatives to do it. They should use base ten blocks, beaded number lines and place value disks. For the visual work, use sketches but also use base ten paper so students can visually see the problems. It is also very important that students can verbalize their strategies.

Depth of Knowledge

Depth of Knowledge is a framework that encourages us to ask questions that require that students think, reason, explain, defend and justify their thinking (Webb, 2002). Here is snapshot of what that can look like in terms of place value work (see Figures 7.68 and 7.69).

Figure 7.68 DOK Activities

	What are different strategies and models that we can use to represent numbers in different ways?	What are different strategies and models that we can use to multiply a two-digit number by a one-digit number?	What are different strategies and models that we can use to model rounding?	What are different strategies and models that we can use to divide a two-digit number by a one-digit number?
Dok Level 1 (these are questions where students are required to simply recall/reproduce an answer/do a procedure)	Represent 262 with number name, base ten sketch, expanded form and standard form.	Solve: 3 × 81	Round 287 to the nearest 10 and the nearest 100.	Solve: 64 ÷ 7
Dok Level 2 (these are questions where students have to use information, think about concepts and reason) This is considered a more challenging problem than a level 1 problem.	Can you represent 262 in two different ways with a base ten sketch.	Can you give me 2 ways to multiply 2 × 75?	Can you give me 3 numbers that round to 400?	Can you give me 2 ways to think about 58 ÷ 4?
Dok Level 3 (these are questions where students have to reason, plan, explain, justify and defend their thinking)	Write a 4-digit number. Represent it in 2 different ways with place value disks.	Give me a problem with a 2-digit number multiplied by a one-digit number that has a product between 250 and 300.	Tell me a story where I would need to round something to the nearest ten.	Give me a problem with a 2-digit number divided by a one-digit number that has a quotient between 7 and 9.

Source: A great resource for asking open questions is Marion Small's *Good Questions: Great ways to differentiate mathematics instruction in the standards-based classroom* (2017). Also, Robert Kaplinsky has done a great job in pushing our thinking forward with the Depth of Knowledge Matrices he created. The Kentucky Department of Education also has great DOK Math Matrices.

Figure 7.69 Asking Rigorous Questions

Dok 1	Dok 2 At this level students explain their thinking.	Dok 3 At this level students have to justify, defend and prove their thinking with objects, drawings and diagrams.
What is the answer to ??? Can you model the number? Can you model the problem? Can you identify the answer that matches this equation? How many hundreds, tens and ones are in this number?	How do you know that the equation is correct? Can you pick the correct answer and explain why it is correct? How can you model that problem? What is another way to model that problem? Can you model that on the ....??? Give me an example of a ... type of problem.... Which answer is incorrect? Explain your thinking?	Can you prove that your answer is correct? Prove that... Explain why that is the answer... Show me how to solve that and explain what you are doing.

Key Points

- Representing numbers in many ways
- Rounding to the nearest 10 and 100
- Multiply a 2-digit number by a 1-digit number
- Divide a 2-digit number by a 1-digit number

Chapter Summary

It is important to spend time developing place value throughout the year. At the beginning of the year, be sure to spend a bit of time reviewing the place value standards from second and third grade through energizers and routines. During the first week of school, set up workstations to review the priority place value standards from the years before. Keep those workstations up all year and add the new ones as they are taught. Also be sure to make sure that parents understand what the place value standards are and ways that they can help to develop it. Send home anchor charts and games for homework.

Reflection Questions

1. How are you currently teaching place value lessons?
2. Are you making sure that you do concrete, pictorial and abstract activities?
3. What do your students struggle with the most, and what ideas are you taking away from this chapter that might inform your work around those struggles?

References

Hanich, L., Jordan, N., Kaplan, D., & Dick, J. (2001). Performance across different areas of mathematical cognition in children with learning difficulties. *Journal of Educational Psychology*, *93*(3), 615.

Jordan, N. C., & Hanich, L. B. (2000). Mathematical thinking in second-grade children with different types of learning difficulties. *Journal of Learning Disabilities*, *33*, 567–578.

Kamii, C. (1985). Leading primary education toward excellence: Beyond worksheets and drill. *Young Children*, *40*(6), 3–9.

Kamii, C., & Joseph, L. (1988). Teaching place value and double-column addition. *Arithmetic Teacher*, *35*(6), 48–52.

Kentucky Department of Education. (2007). *Support materials for core content for assessment version 4.1 mathematics*. Retrieved January 15, 2017.

Miura, I., Okamoto, Y., Chungsoon, K., & Steere, M. (1993). First graders' cognitive representations of understanding of place value: Cross-national comparisons: France, Japan, Korea, Sweden, and the United States. *Journal of Educational Psychology*, *85*(1), 24–30.

Moeller, K., Pixner, S., Zuber, J., Kaufmann, L., & Nuerk, H. C. (2011). Early place-value understanding as a precursor for later arithmetic performance—a longitudinal study on numerical development. *Research in Developmental Disabilities*, *32*(5), 1837–1851.

National Council of Teachers of Mathematics. (2000). *Principles and standards for school mathematics*. Reston, VA: National Council of Teachers of Mathematics.

National Council of Teachers of Mathematics (NCTM). (2006). *Curriculum focal points for prekindergarten through grade 8 mathematics: A quest for coherence*. Reston, VA: NCTM.

National Research Council. (2009). Mathematics learning in early childhood paths toward excellence and equity. In C. T. Cross, T. Woods, & H. Schweingruber (Eds.), *Committee on early childhood mathematics, center for education, division of behavioral and social sciences in education* (pp. 1–386). The National Academies Press.

Sherman, H. J., Richardson, L. I., & Yard, G. J. (2013). *Teaching learners who struggle with mathematics: Systematic intervention and remediation*. Boston, MA: Pearson.

Small, M. (2017). *Good questions: Great ways to differentiate math in the standards based classroom*. New York: Teachers College Press.

Webb, N. (2002). *An analysis of the alignment between mathematics standards and assessments for three states*. Paper presented at the annual meeting of the American Educational Research Association, New Orleans, LA.

8

Fraction Guided Math Lessons

Worldwide, students have trouble with fractions. Yet, fractions are foundational to understanding other aspects of mathematics. Researchers emphasize the key to getting students to understand fractions is to build on conceptual understanding. If students have conceptual understanding, then when they have to learn and use procedural knowledge it makes it that much easier because they understand what they are doing.

In the primary grades, the conceptual understanding foundation is being laid. In third grade, there must be an emphasis on understanding fractions as equal sized pieces of a whole, plotting a fraction on a number line and beginning concepts of equivalence. In fourth grade, students learn to compose and decompose fractions, add and subtract them with the same denominator, find equivalent fractions and in some states students also learn to multiply them by whole numbers. When the emphasis is not placed on the teaching and learning of fractions, students walk away with misunderstandings and misconceptions that grow and impede the learning of more difficult fraction concepts in later grades. One of the biggest misconceptions that students carry with them is viewing the numerator and the denominator as separate numbers rather than 1 number.

Research shows that young children can understand basic fraction concepts such as sharing and the size of fractions when they are set in real-life contexts. Given real contexts, students can develop a fundamental understanding of ordering fractions and equivalence in third grade and solidifying this understanding of these concepts in fourth grade. It is very important to contextualize the discussion about fractions so that students have stories to understand the concepts. We must try to connect students' "intuitive knowledge to formal fraction concepts" (Fazio & Seigler, n.d.).

It is also important to start introducing formal fraction names and attach them to the models and have students do drawings and sketches of these fractions with labels. Fraction notation is important, and we don't want students to be afraid of it, so we should give them plenty of opportunities to write and name the fractions. We should spend a great deal of time building conceptual understanding by doing measurement activities and number lines and comparing activities based on real-life situations. We can use measuring string for jewelry making, talking about sharing food and using rulers. We can use measuring cups, measuring tapes and rulers to model real-life situations.

DOI: 10.4324/9781003169581-8

In this chapter, we will explore:

♦ Composing and decomposing fractions
♦ Adding fractions with like denominators
♦ Subtracting fractions
♦ Multiplying a fraction by a whole number (see Figures 8.1 to 8.57)

Composing and Decomposing Fractions

Overview

Figure 8.1 Overview

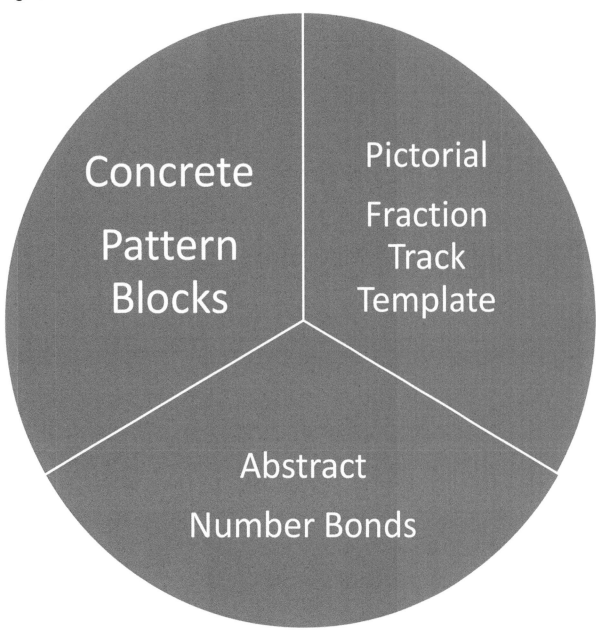

Figure 8.2 Planning Template

Composing and Decomposing Fractions

Big Idea: Numbers, Equivalence, Operation Meanings and Relationships **Enduring Understanding:** Students will understand that fractions can be composed and decomposed in many different ways. **Essential Question:** Why are fractions important? How do we use them in real life? **I can statement:** I can compose and decompose fractions in many different ways.	**Materials** ♦ Tools: Fraction Strips, Pattern Blocks ♦ Templates: Fraction Strip Template ♦ Crayons ♦ Paper

Cycle of Engagement

Concrete:

(EAI)

Pictorial:

1 Whole			
½		½	
1/3	1/3		1/3
1/4	1/4	1/4	1/4

Abstract:

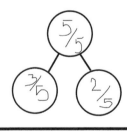

Vocabulary & Language Frames

Vocabulary: whole, halves, thirds, fourths, sixths, eighths, compose, decompose, break apart, number bond

Math Talk:
___ and ___ make ____
___ can decompose into ____ and ____.

Math Processes/Practices
♦ Problem Solving
♦ Reasoning
♦ Models
♦ Tools
♦ Precision
♦ Structure
♦ Pattern

Figure 8.3 Differentiation

3 Differentiated Lessons		
In this series of lessons, students are working on decomposing fractions. They are developing this concept through concrete activities, pictorial activities and abstract activities. Here are some things to think about as you do these lessons.		
Emergent	**On Grade Level**	**Above Grade Level**
Do a lot of work with students looking at fraction strips and where the fractions are on the number line.	Do a lot of work with different manipulatives. Students should use pattern blocks, fraction strips, fraction squares, number lines and other tools.	Work with more denominators.

 Looking for Misunderstandings and Common Errors

This is a tricky skill for many students. The way they learn is to work with manipulatives and have the students to discuss how to break apart these fractions.

Figure 8.4 Anchor Chart

Fraction Strips

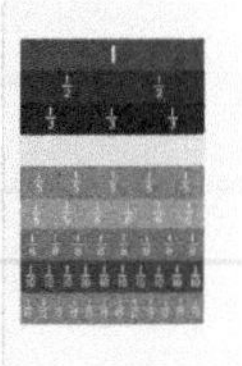

Fraction Strip Template

1 Whole			
½		½	
1/3	1/3		1/3
1/4	1/4	1/4	1/4

Abstract

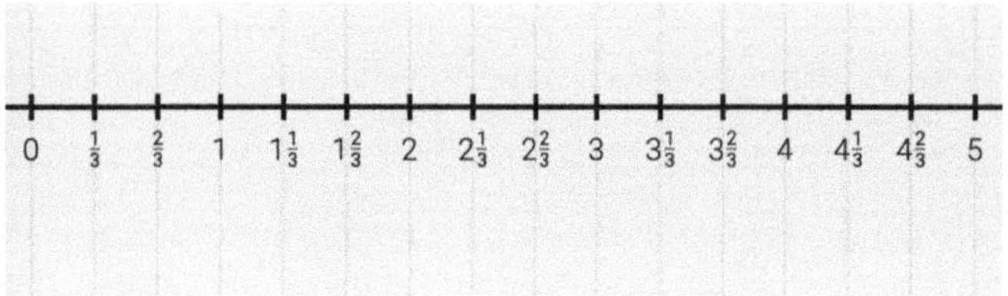

Concrete Lesson

Figure 8.5 Introduction to Concrete Lesson

Introduction to Concrete Explorations

Launch	• **Teacher:** Today we are going to work on using pattern blocks to decompose fractions. • **Vocabulary:** fractions, numerator, denominator, decompose, break apart • **Math Talk:** ____ and ___ make ____ ____ can decompose into ____ and ____
Model	**Teacher:** Today we are going to use pattern blocks to look at how you can break apart a fraction. Let's take a look. I have 3/3. How might I break it apart? What do you see? **Carl:** I see 2/3 plus 1/3. **Tami:** I see 1/3 plus 1/3 plus 1/3
Checking for Understanding	**Teacher:** Let's look at another one. **Terri:** I see 3/6 plus 3/6. **Lucy:** I see 2/6 plus 4/6.

Figure 8.6 Student Activity

	Concrete Student Activity
Guided Practice/ Checking for Understanding	**Teacher:** Let's look at another one. Here is 4/4. How could you break it apart? **Jamal:** I see 2/4 and 2/4. 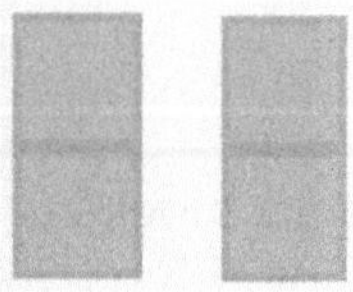 **Hong:** I see ¾ and ¼. 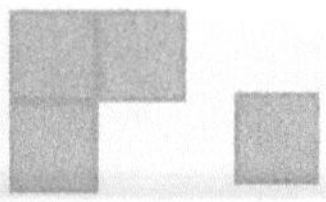
Set up for Independent Practice	Every child gets to share out their thinking about decomposing a fraction and how they reasoned about it. We are going to be talking more about this in the upcoming days. Are there any questions? What was interesting today? What was tricky?

Figure 8.7 Lesson Close

Close
• What did we do today? • What was the math we were practicing? • What were we doing with our pattern blocks? • Was this easy or tricky? • Turn to a partner and state one thing you learned today.

Visual Lesson

Figure 8.8 Visual Introduction

Introduction to Visual Explorations

Launch	**Teacher:** Today we are going to work on using fraction strip templates to decompose fractions. **Vocabulary:** fractions, numerator, denominator, decompose, break apart **Math Talk:** ____ and ___ make ____ ____ can decompose into ____ and ____
Model	**Teacher:** How do you think we might use this to decompose the fractions? **Frankie:** We can see the fraction parts. Like 4/4's. We can break it apart into 2/4 and 2/4.

<table>
<tr><td colspan="4">1 Whole</td></tr>
<tr><td colspan="2">½</td><td colspan="2">½</td></tr>
<tr><td>1/3</td><td>1/3</td><td colspan="2">1/3</td></tr>
<tr><td>1/4</td><td>1/4</td><td>1/4</td><td>1/4</td></tr>
</table>

Checking for Understanding	**Mimi:** We could break it apart into 3/4s and ¼.

<table>
<tr><td colspan="4">1 Whole</td></tr>
<tr><td colspan="2">½</td><td colspan="2">½</td></tr>
<tr><td>1/3</td><td>1/3</td><td colspan="2">1/3</td></tr>
<tr><td>1/4</td><td>1/4</td><td>1/4</td><td>1/4</td></tr>
</table>

Teacher: I am going to give each one of you a problem. I want you to practice representing it with your sketches. Then, you will explain what you did. Who wants to go first?

Figure 8.9 Student Activity

	Visual Student Activity
Guided Practice/ Checking for Understanding	**Teacher:** Who wants to go next? Let's look 3/3's. **Ted:** We could break it apart into 1/3 and 2/3's. | 1 Whole			| |---|---|---|---| | ½ | ½ | | 1/3 | 1/3 | 1/3 | | 1/4 | 1/4 | 1/4 | 1/4 |
Set up for Independent Practice	*Teacher gives everybody a chance to do and discuss a problem. After everyone has shared the lesson ends.* We are going to be talking more about this in the upcoming days. Are there any questions? What was interesting today? What was tricky?

Figure 8.10 Lesson Close

Close
• What did we do today? • What was the math we were practicing? • What were we doing with our fraction strip templates? • Was this easy or tricky? • Turn to a partner and state one thing you learned today.

Figure 8.11 Fraction Strip Template

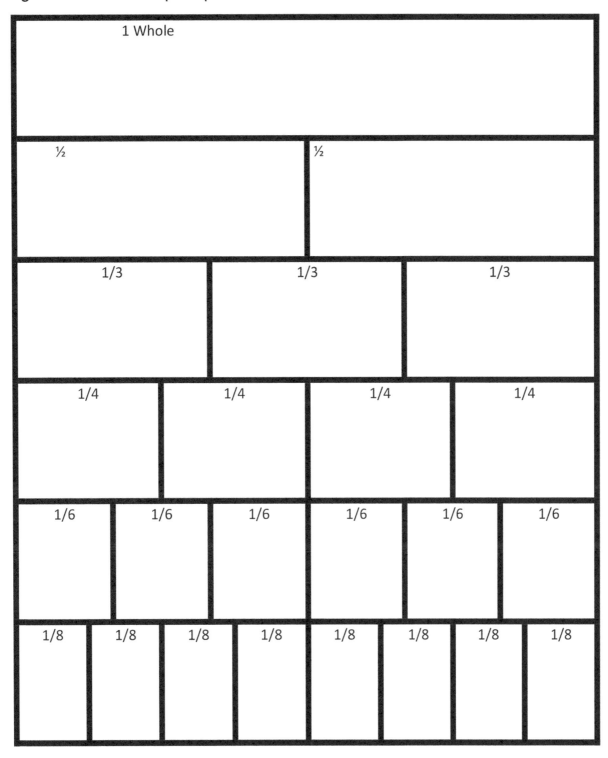

Abstract Lesson

Figure 8.12 Abstract Introduction

Introduction to Abstract Explorations

Launch	**Teacher:** Today we are going to work on using number bonds to break apart fractions. **Vocabulary:** fractions, numerator, denominator, decompose, break apart **Math Talk:** _____ and ___ make _____ _____ can decompose into _____ and _____
Model	**Teacher:** Who can tell me how we might write a way to decompose 5/5? **Dan:** I did this. 5/5 can be broken into 4/5 and 1/5. 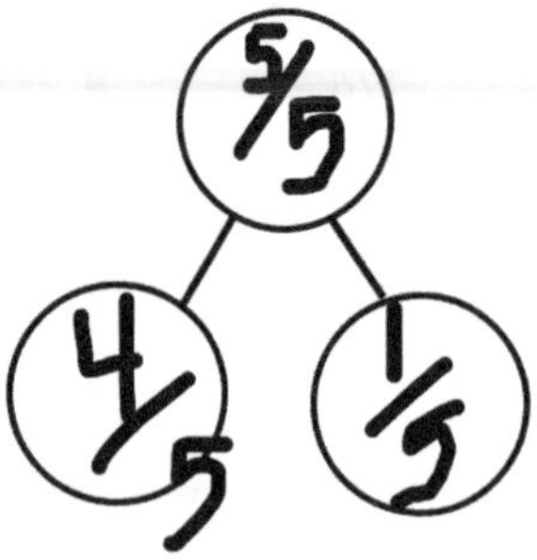
Checking for Understanding	**Teacher:** Who has another way? **Jimmy:** I did 2/5 and 3/5. 

Figure 8.13 Student Activity

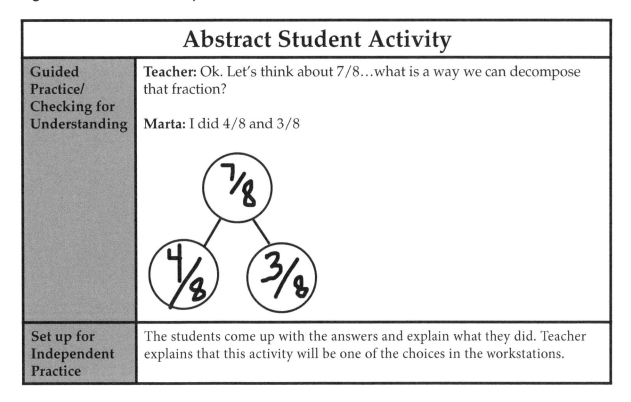

	Abstract Student Activity
Guided Practice/ Checking for Understanding	**Teacher:** Ok. Let's think about 7/8...what is a way we can decompose that fraction? **Marta:** I did 4/8 and 3/8
Set up for Independent Practice	The students come up with the answers and explain what they did. Teacher explains that this activity will be one of the choices in the workstations.

Figure 8.14 Lesson Close

Close
• What did we do today? • What was the math we were practicing? • What were we doing with our number bonds? • Was this easy or tricky? • Turn to a partner and state one thing you learned today.

Section Summary

Decomposing fractions is a very important concept. It lays the foundation for adding fractions. So there should be more time spent on this concept than there usually is. If you do this well, then students will have no problem adding fractions with like denominators. They also will be more flexible with fractions in general for some of the more sophisticated operations. Use a variety of manipulatives to practice decomposing fractions such as pattern blocks, fraction strips, fraction squares and fraction circles. Also use the templates of these manipulatives so that students have more opportunities to visualize what they are doing.

Adding Fractions With Like Denominators

Overview

Figure 8.15 Overview

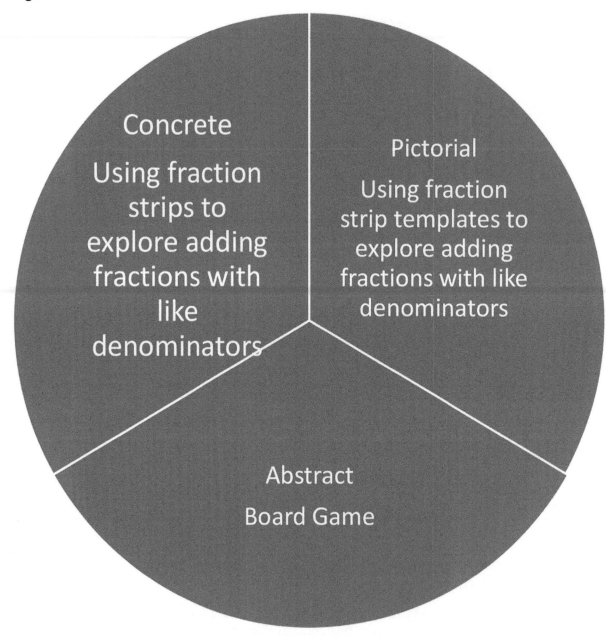

Concrete

Using fraction strips to explore adding fractions with like denominators

Pictorial

Using fraction strip templates to explore adding fractions with like denominators

Abstract

Board Game

Figure 8.16 Planning Template

Adding Fractions with Like Denominators

Big Idea: Numbers; Operation Meaning and Relationships **Enduring Understanding:** Students will understand how to add fractions with like denominators. **Essential Question:** Why are fractions important? How do we use them in real life? **I can statement:** I can discuss and model adding fractions with like denominators.	**Materials** ♦ Tools: Fraction Strips ♦ Templates: Fraction Strip Template ♦ Crayons ♦ Paper

Cycle of Engagement

Concrete:

(EAI)

Pictorial:

1 Whole			
½		½	
1/3	1/3		1/3
1/4	1/4	1/4	1/4

Abstract:

½ + ½ = 1

Vocabulary & Language Frames

Vocabulary: whole, halves, thirds, fourths, sixths, eighths, numerator, denominator, sum, addends,

Math Talk:
___ and ___ make ____
___ can decompose into ____ and ____.

Math Processes/Practices
♦ Problem Solving
♦ Reasoning
♦ Models
♦ Tools
♦ Precision
♦ Structure
♦ Pattern

Figure 8.17 Differentiation

3 Differentiated Lessons

In this series of lessons, students are working on understanding adding fractions with a like denominator. They are developing this concept through concrete activities, pictorial activities and abstract activities. Here are some things to think about as you do these lessons.

Emergent	On Grade Level	Above Grade Level
Students should work with different models, including fraction circles, squares and strips.	Students should use models to understand how to add fractions with like denominators.	Students should work with larger denominators.

 Looking for Misunderstandings and Common Errors

Students will often add both the numerators and the denominators. Use manipulatives to reinforce the concept of adding fractions with like denominators.

Figure 8.18 Anchor Chart

Concrete
(EAI)

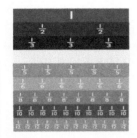

Pictorial:

1 Whole			
½		½	
1/3		1/3	1/3
1/4	1/4	1/4	1/4

Abstract:

¼ + ¼ = 2/4

Concrete Lessons

Figure 8.19 Concrete Introduction

	Introduction to Concrete Explorations
Launch	**Teacher:** Today we are going to work on using fraction strips to think about adding fractions that have the same denominator.
	Vocabulary: fractions, benchmark fractions, halves, thirds, fourths, whole, equivalent, sum, decompose, numerator, denominator
	Math Talk:
	____ and ____ make ____.
Model	**Teacher:** Here we are going to work with fraction strips. I just want you to tell me how we might use these to add fractions.
	Katie: I notice that we could add 1/3 plus 2/3. And that makes 3/3.
	Mark: I notice that if I add 2/5 plus 1/5 that I get 3/5.
	Kenny: I see that 2/6 plus 3/6 is 5/6.
Checking for Understanding	**Teacher:** Ok. We are going to explore some more fractions.

Figure 8.20 Student Concrete Activity

	Concrete Student Activity
Guided Practice/ Checking for Understanding	**Teacher:** We are adding fractions of the same size.
	Teacher: Who wants to go next?
	Mary: I do. I see 2/8 plus 3/8 is 5/8.
Set up for Independent Practice	**Teacher:** How is this tool helping us to add fractions? What do you notice about the fractions we are adding?
	Mary: We can see them.
	Teacher: We are going to be talking more about this in the upcoming days. Are there any questions? What was interesting today? What was tricky?

Figure 8.21 Lesson Close

Close
• What did we do today? • What was the math we were practicing? • What were we doing with our fraction strips? • Was this easy or tricky? • Turn to a partner and state one thing you learned today.

Visual Lessons

Figure 8.22 Visual Introduction

	Introduction to Visual Explorations
Launch	**Teacher:** Today we are going to work on using fraction strips templates to think about adding fractions that have the same denominator. **Vocabulary:** fractions, benchmark fractions, halves, thirds, fourths, whole, equivalent, sum, decompose, numerator, denominator **Math Talk:** ____ and ____ make ____.
Model	**Teacher:** Here we are going to work with fraction strips templates. I just want you to tell me how we might use these to add fractions. <table><tr><td colspan="4">1 Whole</td></tr><tr><td colspan="2">½</td><td colspan="2">½</td></tr><tr><td>1/3</td><td colspan="2">1/3</td><td>1/3</td></tr><tr><td>1/4</td><td>1/4</td><td>1/4</td><td>1/4</td></tr></table> **Jack:** I know one. 2 halves are also equal to 1 whole!
Checking for Understanding	**Teacher:** Yes. Who sees another one? **Ted:** I do. I see ¼ plus ¾ is 4/4. **Tami:** I see 1/3 plus 1/3 is 2/3. **Teacher:** Yes. Who sees another one? **Yesenia:** I could add 3/6 and 1/6 and get 4/6. **Kenny:** I see that 2/6 plus 3/6 is 5/6.

Figure 8.23 Student Activity

	Visual Student Activity
Guided Practice/ Checking for Understanding	**Teacher:** How is this tool helping us to add fractions? What do you notice about the fractions we are adding. **Mary:** We can see the fractions. **Teacher:** We are adding fractions of the same size. **Teacher:** Who wants to go next? **Mary:** I do. I see 2/8 plus 3/8 is 5/8.
Set up for Independent Practice	After all the students share, the teacher wraps up the lesson and the students go to their workstations.

Figure 8.24 Lesson Close

Close
• What did we do today? • What was the math we were practicing? • What were we doing with our fraction strip template? • Was this easy or tricky? • Turn to a partner and state one thing you learned today.

Abstract Lessons

Figure 8.25 Abstract Introduction

Introduction to Visual Explorations

Launch	**Teacher:** Today we are going to play a fraction board game. **Vocabulary:** fractions, benchmark fractions, halves, thirds, fourths, whole, equivalent, sum, decompose, numerator, denominator **Math Talk:** ____ and ____ make ____.
Model	**Teacher:** We are going to play a board game where you are going to add fractions. You all know the rules for playing a board game. Spin the spinner and whoever has the highest number goes first. When you go around the board, you will land on an expression and answer the problem. If you are correct, you stay there. If you are incorrect, you move back a space. Whoever reaches Finish first wins the game. 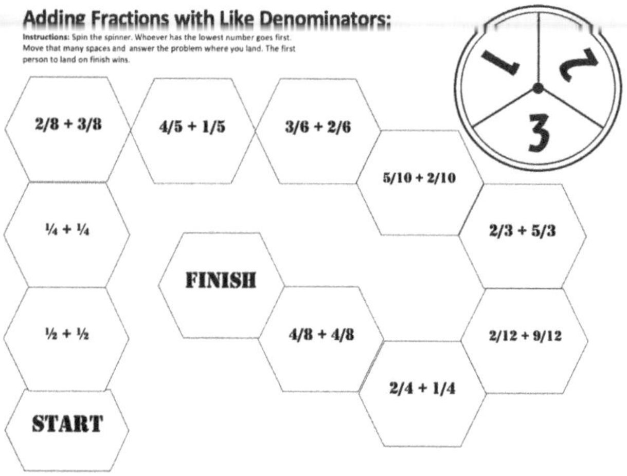 **Adding Fractions with Like Denominators:** Instructions: Spin the spinner. Whoever has the lowest number goes first. Move that many spaces and answer the problem where you land. The first person to land on finish wins. $2/8 + 3/8$ $4/5 + 1/5$ $3/6 + 2/6$ $5/10 + 2/10$ $1/4 + 1/4$ FINISH $2/3 + 5/3$ $1/2 + 1/2$ $4/8 + 4/8$ $2/12 + 9/12$ $2/4 + 1/4$ START
Checking for Understanding	**Teacher:** Does everybody understand what we are going to do? Students shake their heads and say yes.

Figure 8.26 Student Activity

Abstract Student Activities	
Guided Practice/ Checking for Understanding	Teacher watches the partners play games and takes notes and asks the students questions. **Teacher:** Tamia and Hong tell me about your problems. **Tamia:** I landed on 4/5 plus 1/5 and that makes 5/5 which is 1 whole. **Hong:** I landed on 3/6 plus 2/6 and that makes 5/6. You only add the numerators.
Set up for Independent Practice	Every child shares out some of their work. **Teacher:** We are going to be talking more about this in the upcoming days. Are there any questions? What was interesting today? What was tricky?

Figure 8.27 Lesson Close

Close
• What did we do today? • What was the math we were practicing? • What were we doing with our fraction game? • Was this easy or tricky? • Turn to a partner and state one thing you learned today.

Figure 8.28 Addition Gameboard

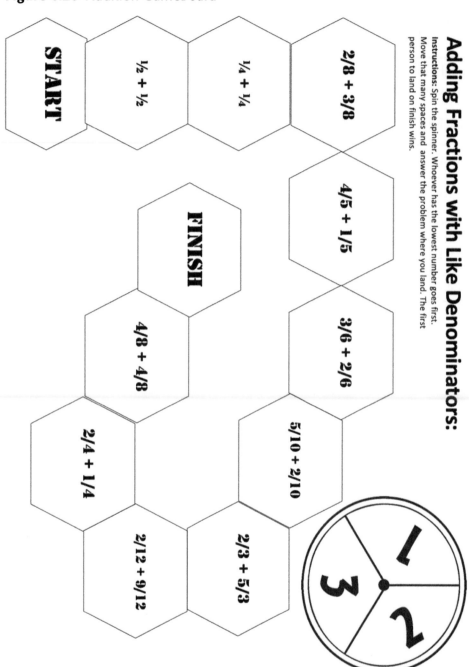

Adding Fractions with Like Denominators:

Instructions: Spin the spinner. Whoever has the lowest number goes first. Move that many spaces and answer the problem where you land. The first person to land on finish wins.

START

½ + ½

¼ + ¼

2/8 + 3/8

4/5 + 1/5

3/6 + 2/6

5/10 + 2/10

2/3 + 5/3

2/12 + 9/12

2/4 + 1/4

4/8 + 4/8

FINISH

Section Summary

Adding fractions needs to be taught with different models such as fraction strips, squares and circles. After students do a great deal of work with the concrete manipulatives, then they should do work with the templates of these manipulatives. When students can model their thinking with concrete and paper manipulatives as well as sketch out their thinking then start playing games where they have to add the fractions with just the numbers.

Subtracting Fractions

Overview

Figure 8.29 Overview

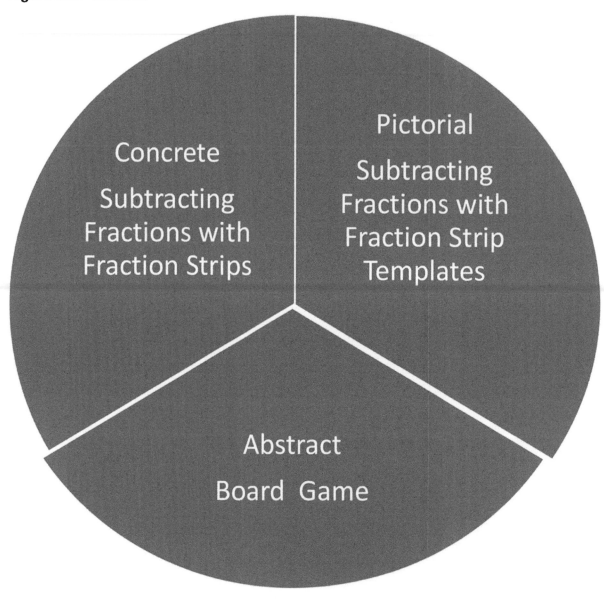

Figure 8.30 Planning Template

Subtracting Fractions with Like Denominators

Big Idea: Numbers; Operation Meaning and Relationships **Enduring Understanding:** Students will understand how to subtract fractions with like denominators. **Essential Question:** Why are fractions important? How do we use them in real life? **I can statement:** I can discuss and model subtracting fractions with like denominators.	**Materials** ♦ Tools: Fraction Strips ♦ Templates: Fraction Strip Template ♦ Crayons ♦ Paper

Cycle of Engagement

Concrete:

(EAI)

Pictorial:

1 Whole			
½		½	
1/3	1/3		1/3
1/4	1/4	1/4	1/4

Abstract:

¾ − ¼ = 2/4

Vocabulary & Language Frames

Vocabulary: whole, halves, thirds, fourths, sixths, eighths, numerator, denominator, sum, addends,

Math Talk:
___ and ___ equal ____.

The sum of ___ and ____ is _____.

Math Processes/Practices
♦ Problem Solving
♦ Reasoning
♦ Models
♦ Tools
♦ Precision
♦ Structure
♦ Pattern

Figure 8.31 Differentiation

3 Differentiated Lessons
In this series of lessons, students are working on the concept of subtracting fractions with like denominators. They are developing this concept through concrete activities, pictorial activities and abstract activities. Here are some things to think about as you do these lessons.

Emergent	On Grade Level	Above Grade Level
Students should work with manipulatives to subtract fractions with like denominators.	Students work with specific denominators in most states: halves, fourths, eighths, thirds, sixths, tenths and twelfths.	Students should work with fractions with a larger denominator.

 Looking for Misunderstandings and Common Errors

Students should do a great deal of work with manipulatives so they understand what they are doing.

Figure 8.32 Anchor Chart

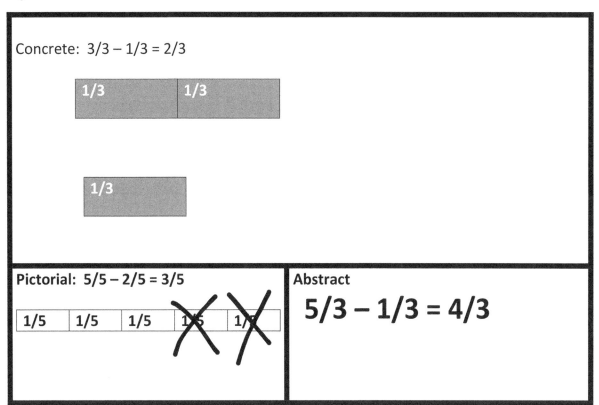

Concrete: 3/3 – 1/3 = 2/3

| 1/3 | 1/3 |

| 1/3 |

Pictorial: 5/5 – 2/5 = 3/5

| 1/5 | 1/5 | 1/5 | 1/5 | 1/5 |

Abstract

5/3 – 1/3 = 4/3

Concrete Lessons

Figure 8.33 Concrete Introduction

<table>
<tr>
<td colspan="2" align="center"><h2>Introduction to Concrete Explorations</h2></td>
</tr>
<tr>
<td>Launch</td>
<td>Teacher: Today we are going to work on using fraction strips to think about subtracting fractions that have the same denominator.

Vocabulary: fractions, benchmark fractions, halves, thirds, fourths, whole, equivalent, numerator, denominator, subtract, minuend, subtrahend, difference

Math Talk:
____ and ____ make ____.</td>
</tr>
<tr>
<td>Model</td>
<td>Teacher: Here we are going to work with fraction strips. I just want you to tell me how we might use these to subtract fractions.

Katie: Say we had 2/3. We could take away 1/3 and we would have 1/3 left.

Mark: I notice that if I had 4/8, I could take away 3/8 and I would have 1/8 left.

Kenny: I see that 5/6 minus 3/6 is 2/6.</td>
</tr>
<tr>
<td>Checking for Understanding</td>
<td>Teacher: Teacher: How is this tool helping us to subtract fractions? What do you notice?

Mary: We can see the fractions.

Teacher: We are taking away fractions of the same size.

Teacher reads 2 more problems that the group discusses.

Teacher: Ok. I am going to give each one of you your own problem. I want you to read it. Solve it. Be ready to share how you did it. I am going to watch you and if you need help, look at our anchor charts and of course you can ask me.</td>
</tr>
</table>

Figure 8.34 Student Activities

	Concrete Student Activities	
Guided Practice/ Checking for Understanding	**Teacher:** Who wants to go next? **Mary:** I do. I see 8/8. If I take away 5/8 then I have 3/8 left. **Tim:** I see 3/5. If I take away 2/5 I have 1/5 left.	
Set up for Independent Practice	Every child shares out their problem and how they solved it using fraction strips. We are going to be talking more about this in the upcoming days. Are there any questions? What was interesting today? What was tricky?	

Figure 8.35 Lesson Close

Close
• What did we do today?   • What was the math we were practicing?   • What were we doing with our fraction strips?   • Was this easy or tricky?   • Turn to a partner and state one thing you learned today.

Figure 8.36 Visual Introduction

Introduction to a Visual Explorations

Launch	**Teacher:** Today we are going to work on using fraction strip templates to think about subtracting fractions that have the same denominator. **Vocabulary:** fractions, benchmark fractions, halves, thirds, fourths, whole, numerator, denominator, subtract, minuend, subtrahend, difference **Math Talk:** ____ and ____ make ____.
Model	**Teacher:** Here we are going to work with fraction strip templates. How might we use these to subtract fractions? 	½		½
1/3	1/3	1/3
1/4	1/4	1/4	1/4
1/5	1/5	1/5	1/5	1/5
1/6	1/6	1/6	1/6	1/6	1/6
1/8	1/8	1/8	1/8	1/8	1/8	1/8	1/8 | **Jack:** I know one. 2 halves take away ½ leaves ½. | ½	½
1/3	1/3	1/3
1/4	1/4	1/4	1/4
1/5	1/5	1/5	1/5	1/5
1/6	1/6	1/6	1/6	1/6	1/6
1/8	1/8	1/8	1/8	1/8	1/8	1/8	1/8	

Figure 8.36 (Continued)

	Teacher: Yes. Who sees another one? **Ted:** I do. I see 2/4 take away ¼ leaves ¼. 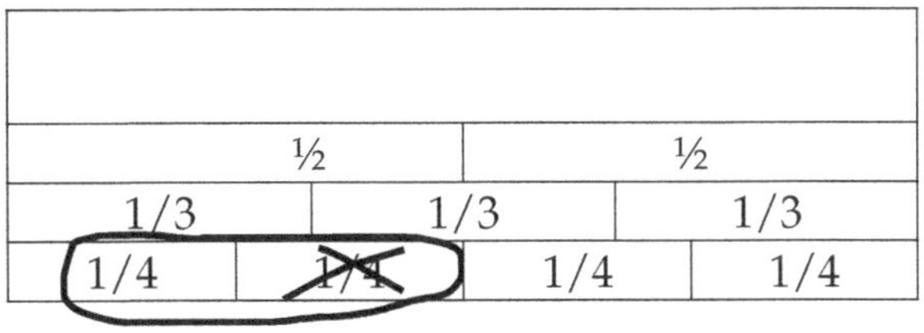
Checking for Understanding	**Micah:** I see 4/5 take away 2/5 is 2/5. 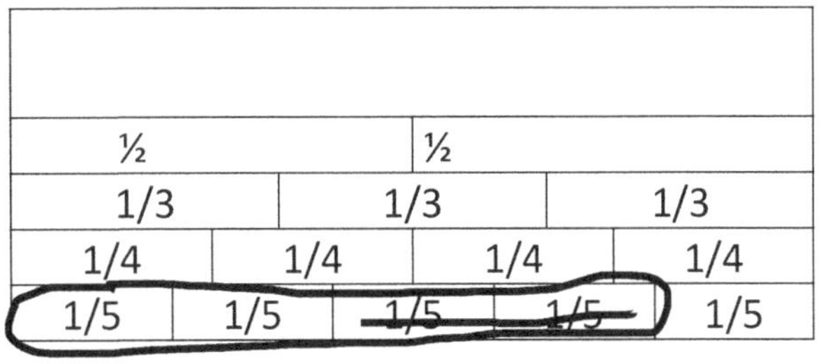

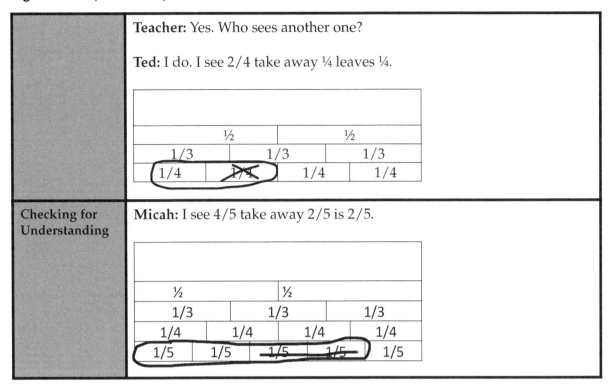

Figure 8.37 Student Activity

	Visual Student Activity
Guided Practice/ Checking for Understanding	**Teacher:** Who sees some other problems? **John:** I do. I see 5/6 minus 2/6 is 3/6. 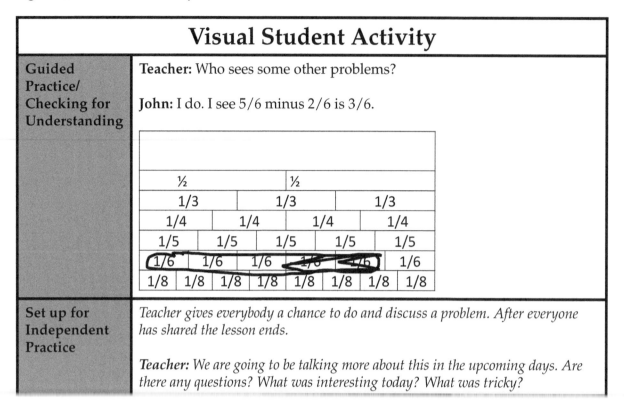
Set up for Independent Practice	*Teacher gives everybody a chance to do and discuss a problem. After everyone has shared the lesson ends.* ***Teacher:*** *We are going to be talking more about this in the upcoming days. Are there any questions? What was interesting today? What was tricky?*

Figure 8.38 Lesson Close

Close
• What did we do today? • What was the math we were practicing? • What were we doing with our fraction strip templates? • Was this easy or tricky? • Turn to a partner and state one thing you learned today.

Figure 8.39 Fraction Strip Template

1							

½	½

1/3	1/3	1/3

1/4	1/4	1/4	1/4

1/5	1/5	1/5	1/5	1/5

1/6	1/6	1/6	1/6	1/6	1/6

1/8	1/8	1/8	1/8	1/8	1/8	1/8	1/8

Abstract Lessons

Figure 8.40 Introduction to Abstract Lesson

	Introduction to Abstract Lesson
Launch	**Teacher:** Today we are going to play a game to practice subtracting fractions that have the same denominator. **Vocabulary:** fractions, benchmark fractions, halves, thirds, fourths, whole, equivalent, numerator, denominator, subtract, minuend, subtrahend, difference **Math Talk:** ____ and ____ make ____.
Model	**Teacher:** We are going to play a board game where you are going to subtract fractions. You all know the rules for playing a board game. Spin the spinner and whoever has the highest number goes first. When you go around the board, you will land on an expression and answer the problem. If you are correct, you stay there. If you are incorrect, you move back a space. Whoever reaches Finish first wins the game. **Subtracting Fractions with Like Denominators:** Instructions: Spin the spinner. Whoever has the lowest number goes first. Move that many spaces and answer the problem where you land. The first person to land on finish wins. 6/8 - 3/8 4/5 - 1/5 3/6 - 2/6 5/10 - 2/10 3/4 + ¼ 2/3 - 1/3 FINISH ½ - ½ 7/8 - 4/8 9/12 - 2/12 7/4 - 3/4 START
Checking for Understanding	**Teacher:** Are there any questions? Ok, let's get started.

Figure 8.41 Student Activity

	Abstract Student Activity
Guided Practice/ Checking for Understanding	Teacher watches the partners play games and takes notes and asks the students questions. **Teacher:** Tracie and Harry tell me about your problems. **Tracie:** I landed on 4/5 minus 1/5 and that leaves 3/5. **Harry:** I landed on 7/4 minus 3/4 and that leaves 4/4. You only subtract the numerators.
Set up for Independent Practice	The teacher watches, listens to and takes notes on the students as they play. She notes who needs more help, who is using the tools and which ones. Then she wraps up the lesson and sends the students to their workstations.

Figure 8.42 Lesson Close

Close
• What did we do today? • What was the math we were practicing? • What were we doing with our fraction game? • Was this easy or tricky? • Turn to a partner and state one thing you learned today.

Figure 8.43 Game Board

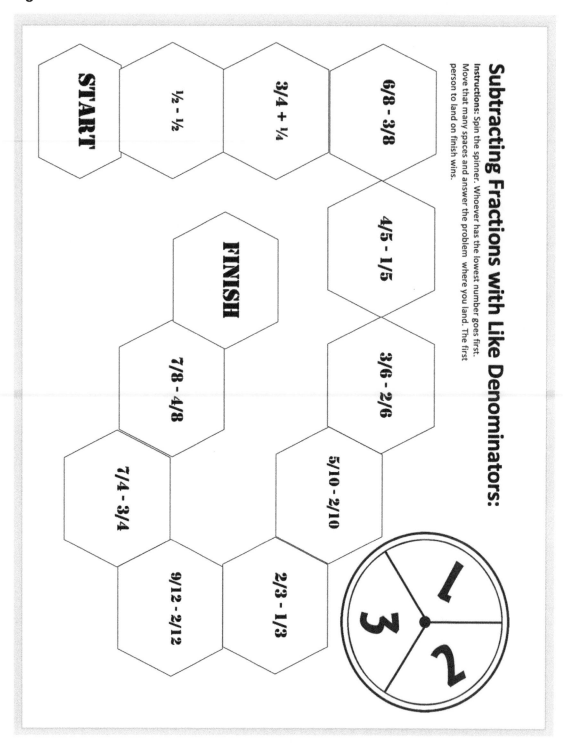

Subtracting Fractions with Like Denominators:

Instructions: Spin the spinner. Whoever has the lowest number goes first. Move that many spaces and answer the problem where you land. The first person to land on finish wins.

START

½ - ½

3/4 + ¼

6/8 - 3/8

4/5 - 1/5

3/6 - 2/6

5/10 - 2/10

2/3 - 1/3

9/12 - 2/12

7/4 - 3/4

7/8 - 4/8

FINISH

1

2

3

Section Summary

Subtracting fractions needs to be taught with different models such as fraction strips, squares and circles. After students do a great deal of work with the concrete manipulatives, then they should do work with the templates of these manipulatives. When students can model their thinking with concrete and paper manipulatives as well as sketch out their thinking, then start playing games where they have to just subtract the fractions.

Multiplying a Fraction by a Whole Number

Overview

Figure 8.44 Overview

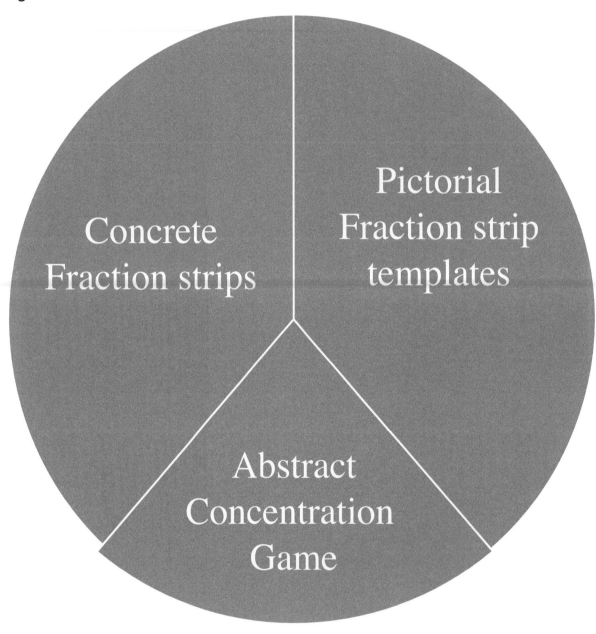

Figure 8.45 Planning Template

Multiplying a Whole Number by a Fraction

Big Idea: Numbers, Operation Meanings and Relationships

Enduring Understanding: Students will understand how to multiply a whole number by a fraction.

Essential Question: Why are fractions important? How do we use them in real life?

I can statement: I can discuss and model multiplying a whole number by a fraction.

Materials
♦ Fraction Strips
♦ Fraction Strip Templates
♦ Fraction Board Game

Cycle of Engagement

Concrete: $4 \times 1/3 = 4/3$

1/3	1/3	1/3	1/3

Pictorial: $6 \times 1/5 = 6/5$

1/5	1/5	1/5	1/5	1/5	**1/5**

Abstract:

$4 \times ½ = 2$

Vocabulary & Language Frames

Vocabulary: whole, halves, thirds, fourths, sixths, eighths

Math Talk:
The fraction of the set is _____

_____ is the fraction of this set

Math Processes/Practices
♦ Problem Solving
♦ Reasoning
♦ Models
♦ Tools
♦ Precision
♦ Structure
♦ Pattern

Figure 8.46 Differentiation

3 Differentiated Lessons		
In this series of lessons, students are working on the concept of multiplying a whole number by a fraction. They are developing this concept through concrete activities, pictorial activities and abstract activities. Here are some things to think about as you do these lessons.		
Emergent	**On Grade Level**	**Above Grade Level**
Most states teach this concept in 4th grade. However a few don't, including Texas.	Students should be able to multiply fractions with specific denominators (usually halves, fourths, thirds, fifths, sixths , tenths, twelfths and eighths).	Expand the range of denominators.

 Looking for Misunderstandings and Common Errors

Use plenty of manipulatives and make the connection between repeated addition and multiplication.

Figure 8.47 Anchor Chart

Concrete: 4 x 1/3 = 4/3

1/3	1/3	1/3	1/3

Pictorial: 6 x 1/5 = 6/5

1/5	1/5	1/5	1/5	1/5	1/5

Abstract:
   4 x ½ = 2

Concrete Lessons

Figure 8.48 Concrete Introduction

Introduction to Abstract Lesson

Launch	**Teacher:** Today we are going to work on using fraction strips to think about multiplying fractions and whole numbers. **Vocabulary:** fractions, benchmark fractions, halves, thirds, fourths, whole, multiply, product, factors **Math Talk:** ___ multiplied by ____ equals ___.
Model	**Teacher:** Here we are going to work with fraction strips. I just want you to tell me how we might use these to multiply fractions. And remember, that multiplying the fractions is just like repeated addition. For example if I say 2 × 1/3 it is the same as 1/3 + 1/3. Who can give me another example? **Ted:** I can think of one. 2 × 1/5 is 1/5 + 1/5 and that would be 2/5. 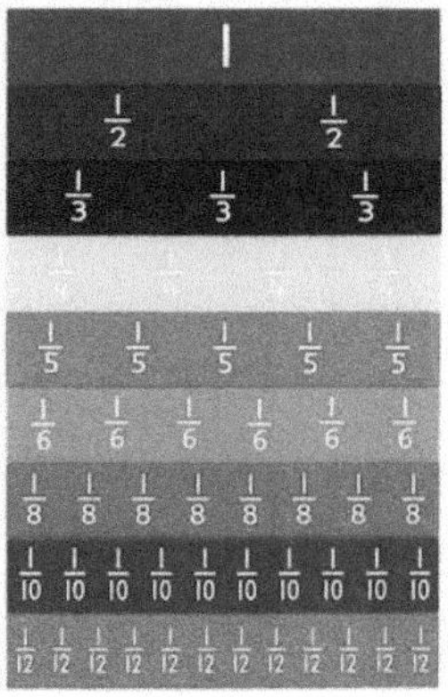
Checking for Understanding	**Marta:** I can think of another one. 3 × 1/3 is going to be 1/3 + 1/3 + 1/3 which is 3/3. **Katie:** I could do 4 × 1/5. So that is 1/5 + 1/5 + 1/5 + 1/5 is 4/5.

Figure 8.49 Student Activity

Concrete Student Activity	
Guided Practice/ Checking for Understanding	**Teacher:** Who has another one? **Tomas:** I can think of another one. 3 × 1/4 is going to be 1/4 + 1/4+ 1/4 which is 3/4. **Katie:** I could do 4 × 1/6. So that is 1/6 + 1/6 + 1/6 + 1/6 which is 4/6.
Set up for Independent Practice	Every child shares out their problem and how they solved it. We are going to be talking more about this in the upcoming days. Are there any questions? What was interesting today? What was tricky?

Figure 8.50 Lesson Close

Close
• What did we do today? • What was the math we were practicing? • What were we doing with our fraction strips? • Was this easy or tricky? • Turn to a partner and state one thing you learned today.

Visual Lessons

Figure 8.51 Visual Introduction

Introduction to a Visual Exploration

Launch	• **Teacher:** Today we are going to work on using fraction strip templates to think about multiplying fractions with whole numbers. • **Vocabulary:** fractions, benchmark fractions, halves, thirds, fourths, whole, numerator, denominator • **Math Talk:** ____ and ____ make ____.
Model	**Teacher:** Here we are going to work with fraction strip diagrams. I just want you to tell me how we might use these to multiply fractions. And remember, that multiplying the fractions is just like repeated addition. So for example if I say $2 \times 1/4$ it is the same as $1/4 + 1/4$. I am going to model it using the diagram. Who can give me another example?

1 Whole								
½				½			
1/3			1/3			1/3	
1/4		1/4		1/4		1/4	
1/5	1/5		1/5	1/5		1/5	
1/6	1/6	1/6	1/6	1/6	1/6		
1/8	1/8	1/8	1/8	1/8	1/8	1/8	1/8

Ray-Ray: I could do $3 \times 1/8$. I would get $1/8 + 1/8 + 1/8$ makes $3/8$. Here is my model.

1 Whole								
½				½			
1/3			1/3			1/3	
1/4		1/4		1/4		1/4	
1/5	1/5		1/5	1/5		1/5	
1/6	1/6	1/6	1/6	1/6	1/6		
1/8	1/8	1/8	1/8	1/8	1/8	1/8	1/8

(Continued)

Figure 8.51 (Continued)

Checking for Understanding	Cynthia: : I could do 2 × 1/3. I would get 1/3 + 1/3 and that makes 2/3. Here is my model. 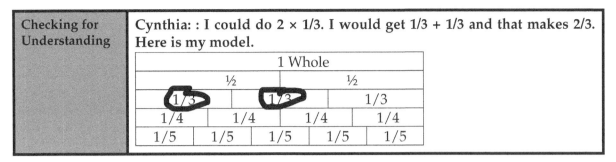

Figure 8.52 Student Activity

Visual Student Activity

Guided Practice/ Checking for Understanding	**Teacher:** Ok, who wants to go next? **Kim:** I could do 2 × 1/6 I would get 1/6 + 1/6 and that makes 2/6. Here is my model.
Set up for Independent Practice	*Teacher gives everybody a chance to do and discuss a problem. After everyone has shared the lesson ends.* We are going to be talking more about this in the upcoming days. Are there any questions? What was interesting today? What was tricky?

Figure 8.53 Lesson Close

Close

- What did we do today?
- What was the math we were practicing?
- What were we doing with our nufraction strip templates?
- Was this easy or tricky?
- Turn to a partner and state one thing you learned today.

Abstract Lessons

Figure 8.54 Abstract Introduction

	Introduction to Abstract Explorations
Launch	**Teacher:** Today we are going to play concentration game to think about multiplying fractions and whole numbers. **Vocabulary:** fractions, benchmark fractions, halves, thirds, fourths, whole, multiply, product, factors **Math Talk:** ___ multiplied by ____ equals ___.
Model	**Teacher:** Today we are going to play a match game where we match the model with the expression. You all know how to play the concentration game…here we are looking for the multiplication equation and the model. **These 2 cards go together because 2 × 1/6 is the same as 1/6 and a 1/6.** 2 x 1/6 | 1/6 | 1/6 |
Checking for Understanding	**Teacher:** Any questions? Ok, let's get started then.

Figure 8.55 Student Activity

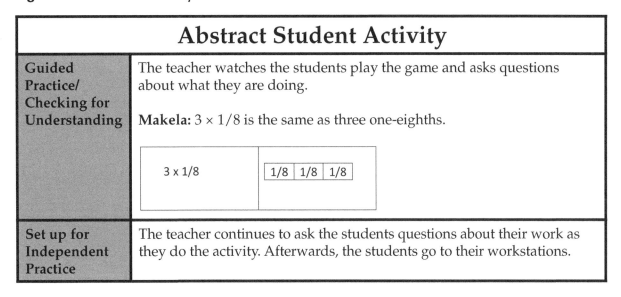

	Abstract Student Activity
Guided Practice/ Checking for Understanding	The teacher watches the students play the game and asks questions about what they are doing. **Makela:** $3 \times 1/8$ is the same as three one-eighths. 3 x 1/8 | 1/8 | 1/8 | 1/8
Set up for Independent Practice	The teacher continues to ask the students questions about their work as they do the activity. Afterwards, the students go to their workstations.

Figure 8.56 Lesson Close

Close
• What did we do today? • What was the math we were practicing? • What were we doing with our concentration game? • Was this easy or tricky? • Turn to a partner and state one thing you learned today.

Figure 8.57 Multiplication Game Cards

2 x 1/8	1/8 + 1/8
3 x 1/5	1/5 + 1/5 + 1/5
4 x 1/2	½ + ½ + ½ + ½
5 x 1/4	¼ + ¼ + ¼ + ¼
3 x 1/2	½ + ½ + ½
2 x 1/10	1/10 + 1/10

Section Summary

Students need a great deal of work to understand multiplying fractions. This should be done through a great deal of model work and the connection between repeated addition and multiplication. We want students to understand what they are doing when they are multiplying and how to model it with different tools. After students have done a great deal of work with concrete models, they should start sketching those models to show their thinking. They should also use visual templates to help them model their thinking as well. Finally, students should play various abstract games to practice multiplying fractions and whole numbers.

Depth of Knowledge

Depth of Knowledge is a framework that encourages us to ask questions that require that students think, reason, explain, defend and justify their thinking (Webb, 2002). Here is snapshot of what that can look like in terms of fraction work (see Figures 8.58 to 8.59).

Figure 8.58 DOK Activities

	What are different ways to decompose a fraction?	What are different ways to add fractions with like denominators?	What are different ways to subtract fractions with like denominators?	What are different ways to multiply a whole number and a fraction?
Dok Level 1 (these are questions where students are required to simply recall/reproduce an answer/do a procedure)	Decompose 5/4.	Solve ¼ + ¼.	Solve 7/8 – 2/8.	Solve 4 × 2/5.
Dok Level 2 (these are questions where students have to use information, think about concepts and reason) This is considered a more challenging problem than a level 1 problem.	Decompose 5/4 in 3 different ways and explain what you did.	Solve ¼ + ¼. Explain and model your thinking.	Solve 7/8 – 2/8. Explain and model your thinking.	Solve 4 × 2/5. Explain and model your thinking.
Dok Level 3 (these are questions where students have to reason, plan, explain, justify and defend their thinking)	Pick your own fraction and decompose it in 3 different ways. Model your thinking.	The answer is 7/8. Tell me 2 different addition fraction expressions that will give this answer.	The answer is 2/6. Tell me 2 different subtraction fraction expressions that will give this answer.	Pick a whole number and a fraction. Multiply it and explain your answer with numbers, words and pictures.

Source: A great resource for asking open questions is Marion Small's *Good Questions: Great ways to differentiate mathematics instruction in the standards-based classroom* (2017). Also, Robert Kaplinsky has done a great job in pushing our thinking forward with the Depth of Knowledge Matrices he created. The Kentucky Department of Education also has great DOK Math Matrices.

Figure 8.59 Asking Rigorous Questions

Dok 1	Dok 2 At this level students explain their thinking.	Dok 3 At this level students have to justify, defend and prove their thinking with objects, drawings and diagrams.
What is the answer to??? Can you model the number? Can you model the problem? Can you identify the answer that matches this equation? How many hundreds, tens and ones are in this number?	How do you know that the equation is correct? Can you pick the correct answer and explain why it is correct? How can you model that problem? What is another way to model that problem? Can you model that on the ....??? Give me an example of a ... type of problem.... Which answer is incorrect? Explain your thinking?	Can you prove that your answer is correct? Prove that... Explain why that is the answer... Show me how to solve that and explain what you are doing.

Key Points

♦ Decomposing fractions
♦ Adding fractions with like denominators
♦ Subtracting fractions with like denominators
♦ Multiplying a fraction by a whole number

Chapter Summary

Teaching fourth grade students about fractions is very important. The work starts in the lower elementary grades, but it is much more formal in third and fourth grade. For students to really grasp the topics they must be introduced at the concrete level. Many books go straight to pictorial representations, but students need plenty of opportunities to manipulate the models. They should use commercial ones, but they should also make their own individual sets of fraction squares, strips and circles. For the circles, it is best to cut out the paper copies so they are sure to be equal parts. Next, students should work on drawing their representations. This takes it to the next level of ownership of the internal knowledge of fractions. Finally, they should be doing abstract work with the symbols. Do not rush to the symbolic representation. Teach fractions all year long through routines and energizers. In the beginning of the year be sure to do energizers and routines with the concepts they learned in the prior grades.

Reflection Questions

1. How are you currently teaching fraction lessons?
2. Are you making sure that you do concrete, pictorial and abstract activities?
3. What do your students struggle with the most, and what ideas are you taking away from this chapter that might inform your work?

References

Empson, S. B. (1999). Equal sharing and shared meaning: The development of fraction concepts in a first-grade classroom. *Cognition and Instruction, 17*, 283–342.

Fazio, L., & Siegler, R. (n.d.). *Teaching fractions.* International Academy of Education & International Bureau of Education.

Kentucky Department of Education. (2007). *Support materials for core content for assessment version 4.1 mathematics.* Retrieved January 15, 2017.

National Council of Teachers of Mathematics. (2007). *The learning of mathematics: 69th NCTM yearbook.* Reston, VA: National Council of Teachers of Mathematics.

Small, M. (2017). *Good questions: Great ways to differentiate math in the standards based classroom.* New York: Teachers College Press.

Vamvakoussi, X., & Vosniadou, S. (2010). How many decimals are there between two fractions? Aspects of secondary school students' understanding of rational numbers and their notation. *Cognition and Instruction, 28*(2), 181–209.

Webb, N. (2002). *An analysis of the alignment between mathematics standards and assessments for three states.* Paper presented at the annual meeting of the American Educational Research Association, New Orleans, LA.
Abstract: This chapter provides an Action Checklist which can be used before, during and after the lessons. Refer to Chapter 3 for Planning Templates to use along with this Action Plan.

9

Action Planning and FAQs

To get started, you must just get started. Pick where you want to start and just begin. Begin small. What follows is an Action Checklist (see Figure 9.1), which can be used before, during and after the lessons. Refer to Chapter 3 for Planning Templates to use along with this Action Plan.

Figure 9.1 Action Checklist

Before the Lesson	
Decide on the topic that you want to do.	
Why are you doing this topic?	
Is this emerging, on grade level or advanced?	
Map out a 3-cycle connected lesson plan.	
What are you going to do concretely?	
What are you going to do pictorially?	
What are you going to do abstractly?	
What misconceptions and error patterns do you anticipate?	
During the Lessons	
What are your questions?	
How are the students doing?	

(Continued)

DOI: 10.4324/9781003169581-9

Figure 9.1 (Continued)

What do you notice?	
What do you hear?	
What do you see?	
After the Lessons	
What went well?	
What will you tweak?	
What will you do the same?	
What will you do differently?	
What made you say "Wow!"	
What made you think "Uh-oh...."	
What did you notice?	
What did you wonder?	
Other Comments	

Frequently Asked Questions

1. **What is a guided math group?**
   Guided math is when you pull a temporary small group of students for instruction around a specific topic. Sometimes the groups are heterogeneous, and sometimes they are homogeneous. It depends on what you are teaching. If you are teaching a specific skill, like rounding, and you have some students who know it and others who are struggling, then you would pull the students who need to learn it into a small group. However, sometimes you are working on general concepts, like solving word problem with models. You can pull a heterogeneous group to teach this.

2. **Why do guided math?**
   You do guided math for a variety of reasons. Lillian Katz said it best:
   When a teacher tries to teach something to the entire class at the same time, chances are, one-third of the kids already know it; one-third will get it; and the remaining third won't. So two-thirds of the children are wasting their time.
   You do guided math so that everyone gets to learn. You can pull students for remedial work, on grade level work and enrichment. You do guided math so that students understand the math they are doing. You work with students in small groups so that they can talk, understand, reason and do math!

3. **What are the types of lessons?**
   There are five types of guided math lessons: conceptual, procedural, reasoning, strategy and disposition. Mostly disposition lessons are integrated throughout the other lessons, but sometimes you just pull students and talk about their journey. That could look like, *what is tricky about what we are learning?* And, *what is easy?*

4. **Do you always use manipulatives in a guided math group?**
   No. It depends where you are in the cycle of developing the concepts and student understanding. You certainly should use manipulatives in the beginning when you are developing concepts, but eventually when students are practicing at the abstract level, they probably won't be working directly with manipulatives, although, sometimes they still use them to check their answers or even solve problems if they need to.

5. **What about doing worksheets in guided math groups?**
   Never. It's simple. Guided math is students doing math, not doing a worksheet. Sometimes, you do pull students to work on some specific problems on a journal page, but that is not the norm or the regular structure of a guided math group.

Reference

Katz, L. Retrieved April 15, 2019 from www.azquotes.com/author/39264-Lilian_Katz

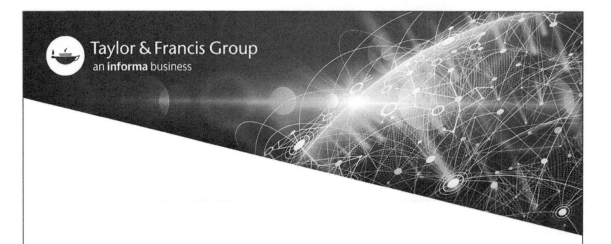

For Product Safety Concerns and Information please contact our EU representative GPSR@taylorandfrancis.com Taylor & Francis Verlag GmbH, Kaufingerstraße 24, 80331 München, Germany

T - #0069 - 090625 - C0 - 280/216/17 - PB - 9780367760021 - Gloss Lamination